PETER CHARLES HOF

The Salem Witchcraft Trials

A Legal History

UNIVERSITY PRESS OF KANSAS

© 1997 by the University Press of Kansas

All rights reserved

Published by the University Press of Kansas (Lawrence, Kansas 66049), which was organized by the Kansas Board of Regents and is operated and funded by Emporia State University, Fort Hays State University, Kansas State University, Pittsburg State University, the University of Kansas, and Wichita State University

Library of Congress Cataloging-in-Publication Data

Hoffer, Peter Charles, 1944–
The Salem witchcraft trials : a legal history / Peter Charles
Hoffer.
p.   cm. — (Landmark law cases & American society)
Includes bibliographical references and index.
ISBN 0-7006-0858-3 (alk. paper). — ISBN 0-7006-0859-1 (pbk.: alk.
paper)
1. Trials (Witchcraft)—Massachusetts—Salem—History.   2. Salem
(Mass.)—History—17th century.   I. Title.   II. Series.
KFM2478.8.W5H645   1997
345.744'50288—dc21   97-19986

British Library Cataloguing in Publication Data is available.

Printed in the United States of America

10 9 8 7 6 5 4 3 2 1

The paper used in this publication meets the minimum requirements of the American National Standard for Permanence of Paper for Printed Materials Z39.48-1984.

CONTENTS

Every society in recorded time has had criminal trials of some kind. These may have been short or long in duration, simple or complex in procedure, based on custom that was passed down orally from generation to generation or based on written rules that only an elite could decipher and apply. A few of these trials have changed the way that people looked at their world. The trial of the "Salem witches" is one of these critical trials.

In the Anglo-American legal tradition, criminal trials have evolved in complexity over the past thousand years. The introduction of trial juries, the appearance of legal counsel for the defense and official (government) prosecutors, and the elaboration of the rights of the accused (so-called procedural guarantees) have transformed criminal trial from an argument between private individuals and their families into a highly formalized function of the state.

The Salem witchcraft trials occurred in the middle of this evolution and exhibit characteristics of both premodern and modern procedures. There were juries, and the government was in charge of the prosecution, but there were no lawyers for the defendants, and the ideal of fair trial was overwhelmed by superstition and rumor. Throughout, the Salem cases were dominated not by book law, that is, written rules scrupulously followed by professional officials of the court, but by folk beliefs shared by the judges, jurors, witnesses, and even the accused. Although common superstitions cannot be kept out of the modern American criminal courtroom, federal and state criminal courts follow highly technical rules of evidence to prevent rumor and hearsay from influencing juries. Indeed, much of what we saw going on in the courtroom during an event like the O. J. Simpson murder trial had to do with the admissibility of evidence.

Conceding the technical differences between trial then and now, there are some powerful similarities. Trial was then and still is an ordeal. Suspects in the Salem cases had to undergo physical examinations for "witch marks" and were made to touch supposed victims. Witch marks were places where the witch's "familiar," usually a small animal, suckled, and touching a victim supposedly lifted the witch's spell. These ordeals were not as severe as those used in medieval England, where reputed witches had to carry a hot iron or survive a dunking in a cold lake, but they had the same root purpose: to put the case before God and seek signs of divine justice.

Today the ordeal is more subtle but just as real. The family of the victim comes to court hoping for retribution. The family of the accused sits on the other side of the courtroom praying for vindication of the defendant's claim of innocence. When the verdict is delivered, one side will weep tears of joy or cry out in long-suppressed triumph; the other side will mourn and swear that injustice has won the day. The trial is also an ordeal for the prosecution and the defense lawyers, whose time and energy it consumes. The patience and wisdom of the judge have been tried, and the time and emotional strength of the jury may be sapped as well.

The point of the ordeal was to seek truth, and truth remains the fundamental objective of a criminal trial. With the introduction of trial juries in the late Middle Ages, trials became a contest to convince jurors that one side's version of the story is correct. At Salem, it is clear that the jurors often did not know whom or what to believe. They were just as frightened of witches and just as credulous about the powers of the Devil as anyone else. These fears were easily manipulated by officials seeking convictions. In some cases the prosecutors wanted political advancement; in others they truly believed that the colony was beset by Satan and His minions. Personal animosity played a role as well.

As Jeremy Bentham, the great English legal reformer of the late eighteenth century, sarcastically noted, such trials were like fox hunts. The defendants were ranged against the government as in a sporting event. The jury heard different versions of the facts from both sides. Bentham did not trust this adversarial method of establishing facts at criminal trials, for it encouraged both sides to use dirty tricks and underhanded methods to convince the jury. At its worst, the contest turned into a combat wherein no holds were barred. Up to Bentham's time, the state had the advantage in the chase. The defendants in the Salem cases had friends and family to give support, but they did not have legal counsel to plead for them, and the judges were not impartial.

Not so today. Our criminal justice system relies for fairness upon procedural guarantees drawn from the federal and state constitutions, like the right to counsel, the right to be free from unlawful searches and seizures, the right to confront accusers, and the right to compel production of evidence that might aid the defense. The state has the burden of proving its case; the defendants do not have to prove their innocence. And, most important, at trial two precepts protect the defendant—the "innocent until proven guilty" rule and the "beyond reasonable doubt" test for a guilty verdict. The watchword of our criminal justice system is that it is better for a hundred guilty people to escape conviction than for one innocent person to be wrongly found guilty. Perhaps the notoriety of the Salem cases was responsible, in some small but palpable way, for the changes between then and now.

ACKNOWLEDGMENTS

In the process of creating this text, I have indebted myself to librarians, archivists, scholars, and publishers, all of whom I wish to thank here. A first version of my inquiry was published under the title *The Devil's Disciples: Makers of the Salem Witchcraft Trials* by the Johns Hopkins University Press. The present book is a distinct work, framed and presented in a different way, but it rests upon the same base of research. I am grateful to the staffs of the Danvers Historical Society; the Essex Institute in Salem, Massachusetts; the Folger Library in Washington, D.C.; the Rare Books Rooms at the Columbia University Library in New York City; the New York University and University of Pennsylvania law libraries; the African Studies Institute at Penn; and the Library System of the University of Georgia. I was able to present portions of the work at the Ethel Wolfe Institute at Brooklyn College, the Columbia University Seminar in Early Modern History, the Rorschach Lecture at Rice University, the legal history seminar at New York University School of Law, and the annual meeting of the American Society for Legal History. I also acknowledge my debt to John Baker, Tim Breen, Richard Godbeer, Natalie Hull, Harold Hyman, Stan Katz, David Konig, Mike McGiffert, Eben Moglen, Bill Nelson, Richard Ross, David Schoenbrun, and Michael Winship, who commented on pieces of various drafts. David McGee checked and rechecked citations. Elaine Breslaw and Tony Phillips shared valuable unpublished material with me.

At the University Press of Kansas, Editor in Chief Mike Briggs, Assistant Director Susan Schott, and Director Fred Woodward have unstintingly supported the series of which this book is a part. I am grateful to my coeditor, N. E. H. Hull, for all her assistance in this and our previous collaborations. David Konig reread the manuscript and saved me from numerous errors. I dedicate the book to little Dorcas Good, long past too late to save her from the persecution of all the witchfinders who saw in the cringing form of a four-year-old girl the shadow of their own devilment and did not recognize its shape.

Introduction

On September 12, 1692, a fourteen-year-old Andover farm boy named William Barker Jr. stood before Essex County, Massachusetts, justices of the peace and stammered out a confession. He had made a pact with the Devil. Six days before, he had stumbled upon a snarling black dog that frightened him, and the next morning a man dressed in the same black made young Barker dip his hand into something red and make his mark in a book. It was the Devil's book, he sobbed, admitting that for a new suit of clothes he had agreed to do the Devil's bidding. With other witches, he gained the power to strike down innocent people with his "evil eye" and to fly upon a pole to join in witches' secret meetings. This he swore, just as his mother and father before him swore, they just as terrified as he of the consequences of not saying whatever their inquisitors wanted to hear.

The four magistrates who took the confession believed the frightened lad. Bartholomew Gedney, Jonathan Corwin, John Hathorne, and Jonathan Higginson were all men of means and experience, but they did not hesitate to credit the boy's tale of wild flights through the winter night to secret gatherings of howling witches. Indeed, in the four months from June through September, nineteen men and women who had professed their innocence were hanged. One stubborn man would not concede that the court could try him; he was pressed to death with heavy stones. Those who confessed, like young Barker, were spared. Was the world turned upside down? It was safer, at least for the time being, for God-fearing, churchgoing men, women, and children to declare that they had met the Devil and bowed to Him than to insist that they remained faithful to the Lord's commandments.

No one knew where it would end. Between January 1692 and May 1693, the men and women of Salem, Massachusetts, and the neighboring towns lived in imminent fear of witches and their master, the Devil.

Hundreds were accused, many of whom languished in jail for months. Neighbor turned against neighbor, children informed on parents, and ministers expelled members of their congregations. Later, when the trials had ended almost as abruptly as they had begun, many swore that the Devil had been among them and had deceived them. Samuel Parris, the minister whose sick child Betty was the first of the girls "bewitched," later concluded that God had "suffered the evil angels to delude us." Thomas Fisk, foreman of one of the Salem trial juries, sobbed, "We confess that we ourselves were not capable to understand the mysterious delusions of the Powers of Darkness, and Prince of the Air . . . whereby we fear we have been instrumental with others, tho ignorantly and unwittingly, to bring upon ourselves and this People of the Lord, the Guilt of Innocent Blood." Surely there was a lesson here; there was always a lesson in God's Providence. As the Reverend Samuel Willard preached on November 27, 1692—after watching the trials closely and grieving aloud that innocent people went to the gallows—"There is a voice in every turn of providence which passeth over men, and it speaks to them, signifying what it is that God requires of them at such a time, and it highly concerns them to hear it, that so they may practice accordingly."

In that year, Providence spoke to the people of New England in fire and brimstone. A brutal, lingering war on the frontier with Canada and Canada's Indian allies had already cost both sides many more lives than were lost in all the witchcraft trials later that year, or in any of the years before it in America. Accompanying the conflict was a crisis within the Massachusetts government, in which a party of local patriots had overthrown the royal officials but not been able to replace them with a stable provincial system. Partisan factions waited for new English monarchs, William and Mary, to approve or disapprove of what the Massachusetts patriots had done. An equally disquieting religious predicament threatened worship in the colony. Attendance at services was falling away, as was some Puritans' desire to seek full membership in their churches. The latter required a confession of faith before the congregation, which many were unwilling or unable to provide. Parris and Willard shared the faith that God had singled out New England, but His will was not plain. Was all the suffering a test of faith or a proof that God had hidden His face from them? Why had such travail befallen them?

Not so long ago, I asked students in my American history survey class if they thought that the American Revolution was inevitable. Almost unanimously they agreed that it was. When I questioned them in the same vein about the direction of their own lives, they vigorously replied that they could choose their own course. In fine, they believed that great events must happen as they did but that individuals were free to make their own history. These are thought-provoking views, for they illuminate a central problem in writing and teaching about the past. As living beings, we assume that our volition plays a part in shaping our lives. We see the effects of our choices every day. Yet somehow, seen from a distance, major historical events lose the quality of human agency and become predetermined by immovable historical forces.

I believe that one task historians can perform for their students, whether in class or in the writing of books for student use, is to recover the element of human choice, of agency, in our account of important events. As the late English labor historian Edward Thompson proposed in the preface to his magnificent *The Making of the English Working Class* (1963): "My quarrel with [earlier accounts of English working people] is that they tend to obscure the agency of working people, the degree to which they contributed, by conscious efforts, to the making of history." History is the story of ordinary people's choices, even when, despite their best efforts, they become nameless victims of war, disease, poverty, and crime.

Nowhere are these suppositions more crucial, and in no subject can they be better tested, than in the Salem witchcraft trials. Overwhelmed by the apparent lack of rationality in the charges made by a handful of girls against so many of their neighbors, appalled at the flimsy evidence offered at the trials and the apparent gullibility of the judges and jurymen, today's students might conclude that the whole episode was merely the product of malign forces of yesteryear. The explanation would go like this: the trials were governed by forces no one could control, a last gasp of superstition in a time when ignorant people believed in the nocturnal flights of woodland fairies and the evil spells of wicked witches. Individual choices were overwhelmed by irresistible forces. Soon the bright rays of the Enlightenment would bring a new age of reason and science to the Western world, and no one in power would give such credence to spectral flights of fancy. In a way, such an explanation echoes the story that the Reverend Parris told at the time. The Devil made him do it. He was powerless before the onslaught of forces greater than any person could resist.

There is truth in the generalization that the people of the seventeenth century were by and large more gullible than their eighteenth-century descendants. In the 1600s, popular or "vernacular" belief in witches was repeated in the writings of the most learned men. Only at the end of the century did people of wealth and education begin to divorce themselves from folk opinion. As cultural historian Peter Burke argued in the last chapter of his much cited *Popular Culture in Early Modern Europe*: "In 1500 . . . popular culture was everyone's culture; a second culture for the educated, and the only culture for everyone else. By 1800, however, in most parts of Europe, the clergy, the nobility, the merchants, the professional men—and their wives—had abandoned popular culture to the lower classes, from whom they were now separated, as never before, by profound differences in world view."

Burke's account of the parting of the ways of the elite and popular culture seems to fit the general chronology of witchcraft persecution in Europe. At first, the well-born and the commoner agreed that witches were abroad and could do evil through spells, curses, and a glance from their "evil eye." Authorities agreed that the malign cunning of witches came from a bargain with Satan. Endemic throughout Europe, the British Isles, and New England in the seventeenth century, prosecution of witches all but disappeared in the next century, as elites in these societies began to doubt that witches had any power at all, except to frighten credulous peasants. Are my students and Samuel Parris then correct? Was the tragedy at Salem inevitable? Did the Salem Villagers simply have the misfortune to live on the exact spot where history's tectonic plates came together and tore the earth above them asunder?

If England had been seized with a mania for prosecution of witches in the late sixteenth and early seventeenth centuries, the people of the Massachusetts Bay Colony were out of step. By 1692 many English judges, scientists, and philosophers had long doubted the efficacy of witchcraft. More concerned about the visible world and its measurable phenomena than the invisible one, with its miracles and prodigies, they required more reasonable proofs of causation than testimony about midnight flights through the air by women on poles. If the number of denunciations remained the same, for the common people clung to the fear of witches, the number of indictments, convictions, and executions plummeted, then ceased—proof that the authorities no longer credited what the common people said they saw. But not quite yet in New England, for there witchcraft continued to plague elite and commoner alike. Every strange cat, menacing dog, eerie crow, and sinister snake cast the shadow of the witch in the folk imagination, and the ministers and magistrates credulously recorded every episode in their diaries and spoke of them in their sermons. All of which means that great transatlantic cultural forces did not dictate the inevitability of the trials in Salem.

Was woman hating another irresistible force that inexorably led to the outbreak of witchcraft in Salem? True, the targets of witchcraft prosecutions were overwhelmingly women, in part because men had fashioned the offense to persecute women. Women who were different, women who would not show submissiveness to men, women who violated the special rules men laid down making women inferior to men in the eyes of the law, the church, and even their neighbors— such women found themselves accused of witchcraft. Men of learning in England and New England agreed: suspected witches were either weak-minded wenches, easily misled by the Great Deceiver, or ill-tempered hags who asked the Devil for assistance. The misogyny of the accounts was integral to their popularity. As English country churchman John Gaule only half joked in 1646: "[E]very old woman with a wrinkled face, a furr'd brow, a hairy lip, a gobber tooth, a squint eye, a squeaking voice, or a scolding tongue . . . and a dog or cat by her side" was in danger of such a charge. He was not joking when he added that "the fittest subjects" for the Devil "are women commonly." Did they not revel in "infirmity, ignorance, impotence of passions and affections, melancholy . . . and vagrant lust"? Minister William Baxter, cited with admiration by New England's leading clergymen, was even more explicit about the gendered nature of witchcraft, in which "lustful, rank girls and young widows that plot for some amorous, procacious design, or have imaginations conquered by lust . . . [there] Satan oft sets in."

Again, stubborn historical fact undermines the easy generalization about misogyny and fears of witches. In New England, women were regarded not as an evil but as a "necessary good." Women were treated better, had more say in their fate, and had better prospects than in the Old World. What is more, in Salem, women were prominent among the accusers as well as the suspects of witchcraft. Men were also accused, and some were convicted of the crime. Although in some cases witchcraft accusations were leveled against women who did not fit in, or who had property that was desired by others, or who struck out at neighbors in their community, the crime of witchcraft was not a male conspiracy against women. In making the female suspect a victim without recourse to her own abilities, skills, or intelligence, we deny the agency of women. They were capable of fighting back, and they did.

By reducing our story to a puppet show, in which superstition and antifeminism by turns manipulate the feelings and acts of the players, we demean the choices made by the accusers, who included some women in their accusations but excluded others. If, in the end, we regard complex human beings as mere pawns of powerful cultural forces, we lose all sense of the importance of choice and contingency. People might have acted differently in Salem than the way they did. There were other times in New England when a witchcraft scare brought out the worst in people, but ministers and judges refused to allow the scare to become a panic. And as important as choice was, contingency was even more critical. In Salem, the completely accidental arrival of a Barbados planter turned merchant turned lay preacher and his African-born Barbadian slave were the reasons the crisis took the form it did. We must try to reconstruct the feelings and understand the actions of people who could and did change their world, initially rendering it a place of suspicion and accusation, then, when they saw what they had wrought, trying to make amends.

———

How can we recover and reassert the human agency of the characters in the Salem trials? One way is to conceptualize the trials as a dramatic performance. As Milner Ball has suggested in a 1975 *Stanford Law Review* article entitled "The Play's the Thing," trials are sources of drama and provide the setting for dramas. The courtroom is a stage, with the chief characters moving about as though they were characters in a play. The judge and jury are the audience; the accusers, accused, and witnesses are the players. Prosecutors and defendants write the lines as they go. There are "props" in both trials and theater—the "exhibits" that are admitted as evidence in court and the paraphernalia of the stage actor. Anyone who reads the records of the pretrial examinations in law cases or consults the eyewitness accounts will be struck by the stagelike quality of the conduct of the accusers.

Criminal trials like those in Salem (and more modern ones, like the Lindbergh kidnapping trial and the O. J. Simpson trial) are popular entertainment as well as deadly serious affairs. Even for those whose lives, fortunes, and credibility hang in the balance of the outcome of the trial, the trial works as theater. It brings the community together like the audience of a play to experience the drama. Trials and theater force an audience to think about its beliefs and values. In the end, like good theater, the trial persuades everyone that justice has been done.

Ironically, the Puritans were dead set against theatrical performances, counting them as occasions for immorality and profligacy. They would not allow "players" or stage troupes to perform in New England, and one suspects they would hotly object to any analogy between the criminal trials in Salem and a theatrical performance. And truth to tell, unlike Ball's ideal trial, the Salem trials did not leave everyone with the sense that justice had been done. Indeed, no sooner were they over than many cried out against them. Today, they have become a metaphor for miscarriage of justice, superstition, and credulity. Mere mention of them calls up the specter of unproved and unprovable aspersions, the presumption of guilt, and the destruction of family and community.

One of the most chilling and brilliant stage plays of the twentieth century focused on the Salem witchcraft trials and captured the danger of false accusations based on rumor and spite. Arthur Miller's play *The Crucible* (1953) not only reminded its audiences of the terrible tragedy at Salem but also warned that "witch-hunts" could begin at any time. Indeed, America was then suffering through a vicious and baseless persecution of many innocent people by a U.S. senator from Wisconsin named Joseph McCarthy and his allies. Miller wrote against them, as well as against the makers of the Salem trials. Although he based his work on the historical record, he took some liberties with the facts. He invented dialogue and changed names, ages, and dates in the furtherance of dramatic effect. Miller wrote the screenplay for the movie version of *The Crucible*, and there took even more liberties with the facts—but he captured on the large screen the sense of panic, outrage, and pathos of the trials. The historian cannot invent facts in this way, but Miller's work is an inspiration to us, for it reminds us that we are not proof against the superstition and rumormongering that brought on the tragedy in Salem.

CHAPTER I

Newcomers on the Road to Salem

The story of the Salem witchcraft trials begins with two newcomers to Salem. The first of these was an Englishman in his midthirties named Samuel Parris. Samuel's family were London merchants and members of a radical Protestant sect. These Puritans, whose origins lay in a late-sixteenth-century reform movement within English Protestantism, were by the 1650s divided into many factions, but all believed that bishops, the mass, and all other remnants of Roman Catholic worship had to be purged from English pulpits. In the 1640s they had taken a leading role in a revolution against royal authority that led to the execution of King Charles I, and in the next decade they participated in the coalition that ruled the realm.

As pious and self-critical as Puritans were, they were not averse to the ways of the marketplace. Seeking wealth, some traveled to England's new colony in the West Indies—Barbados. Samuel's family arrived there sometime in the late 1660s. Barbados, created as an outpost of English military aspirations and commercial enterprise, was transformed twice under English rule in the seventeenth century. Uninhabited when the English arrived in 1624—the Spanish had killed or enslaved its native Taino and Carib population long before—Barbados was soon dotted with tobacco farms. Just as the price of tobacco was falling, the planters, with Dutch help, were able to shift to sugarcane production. Cane sugar was an Asian plant that thrived in the subtropics of the Americas. Every European who loved coffee or tea now found they needed sugar as well, creating a consumer demand unparalleled in its time. Slaves were imported from Africa to join with indentured European servants in the fields and the sugar "factories" of the island. Once rich green from dense woodland, Barbados was denuded of timber—all to feed the fires that boiled down the sugarcane. Wood for building and for fuel had to be imported from

New England. By the 1660s a second revolution had changed the human face of the island from white to black. Slave importation increased, slave gangs became the rule, and local landlords gradually abandoned the island and left the duties of overseeing planting to younger relatives or hired managers.

Samuel Parris's father, Thomas Parris, had made and lost a fortune in real estate and shipping on the island. Eager to escape the risks of sugar planting and the vagaries of sugar prices, he borrowed heavily, invested in slaves, and failed again. His younger son watched. Still, others made fortunes from sugar and rum. One need not have land to become wealthy. With a labor force too large to be fed by native hands, Barbados needed flour and fish. Puritans like the Parrises became middlemen in the trade. Like planting, buying and selling was chancy. Family and friends provided risk capital—but when payments from consignees did not come in, failure, bankruptcy, and disgrace lurked in the blank pages of the ledger book. Life was precarious, precious, and contested, but with careful management and luck a man still could grow rich.

Shortly before Thomas died, he gave to Samuel the gift of an education at Harvard College in Cambridge, Massachusetts. There young Parris went in 1670, accompanied by his father's friend John Oxenbridge. In Cambridge Samuel found not the settled college life that had already produced two generations of ministers for New England pulpits but chaos. Harvard College teetered on the brink of disaster. The number of students had declined, the buildings were in poor repair, and the students were in open rebellion against President Leonard Hoar, who tried to stem the failing college's fortunes by strictly enforcing its rules. Samuel did not stay the course in any case, for in 1673 he received word that his father had died, and he returned to Barbados.

Samuel's sojourn in Cambridge had been a new experience for the young planter, but there is no evidence that because of it Samuel had come to doubt the values or methods of the planter classes. The difficulties of life on the island notwithstanding, he had left a station near the top of Barbadian society and returned to it wiser but not changed. Yet if he was like other Puritan youths who found themselves on the island, he yearned for the comforts of family and church, and if he did not reject the materialism of the countinghouse, he regretted the demands it made upon his spirit. Smaller planters like his father were being inexorably squeezed from their land, and Thomas Parris had already sold off all but one of his farms by the time he died. Disease continued to carry off the Europeans. Slave rebellion, two years in the future, was already feared, and hurricanes had already struck, though the most damaging would come in 1675. Many young men like Parris left the island permanently to seek their fortunes in the mother country or her North American colonies.

Young Parris first tried his hand at bettering his position. Selling off his late father's remaining holdings in the countryside, he set himself up as a merchant in Bridgetown. The port was dominated by its wharves and jetties. From these a maze of streets stretched almost a mile and a half in a crescent along the southwestern, lee shore of the island, between a swamp on the east and a gravelly slope on the west. The climate was tropical, wet, fly-filled in the day and mosquito-ridden at night, but the wharves were crowded with ships, and others waited offshore to dock and take on their cargo of sugar. In the taverns and the countinghouses all classes and races of people mingled.

For merchants and planters, slaves provided a hedge against bankruptcy. They were mobile capital. If they survived the rigors of island life, they could be sold or carried to another, safer, clime. Parris purchased a young slave woman named Tituba as a house servant. She is the second major character in our story. Tituba is a Yoruba name, the language of the people of what was then called the "slave coast" and now comprises parts of Benin, Ivory Coast, and southwestern Nigeria. The Oyo kings of Yorubaland engaged in the slave trade on a large scale. For Africans who owned or traded them, slaves counted as people—inferior people to be sure, but still human. The children of slaves might become full members of the masters' community. For the European buyers, slaves were merely pieces of property to be carried off to plantations in the New World. In effect, slaves had become a kind of currency—a legal tender of war and domination that Africans created and Europeans exploited.

Many of those slaves were carried by local agents to the foreigners' fortress-warehouses on the slave coast. The English maintained such forts along the shore from Senegal in the northwest to the Niger Delta in the southeast, and these had the usual garrison and "trunk" for slaves awaiting shipment across the ocean. There, supercargoes working for British merchants, primarily the Royal African Company, put together cargoes of slaves for the English settlements in the West Indies. On average, about 12 percent of the human cargo died en route, sometimes from disease, sometimes from simply not wanting to live. Suicide was always a problem. Along the coast, Europeans also succumbed to illness. Their average survival rate was one to two years, but some died sooner, and a few survived longer. On board the ships, many sailors and officers died, adding to the cost of the slave trade.

Parris purchased young Tituba and Indian John, the man who later was styled her consort, late in the 1670s. One scholar called Tituba "ageless," suggesting that she was into middle age, thus giving her a haglike visage appropriate for a witch. But if Tituba was in her teens when Parris bought her, she would have been in her twenties in 1692—hardly ancient, although her features might have been prematurely weathered by a life of forced travel and hard labor. Parris would have intentionally bought his slave young, for English masters preferred that slaves be trained within the master's family. When, within three years of arriving, Parris had made up his mind to leave, he took the two slaves, Tituba and Indian John, and sailed for Boston. The travels of these three people were not unusual, for the Atlantic Ocean in the seventeenth century had become a highway over which moved a continuous traffic in goods and people.

Boston was a natural destination for Parris, for not only did the Parris family have dealings there but other Barbadian merchants used Boston as a depot for their exports. In effect, London, Boston, and Bridgetown formed a triangle of trade. Parris was already determined to be a merchant, and his ties were with New England. He was not, however, a New Englander but, for the better part of his life, a Barbadian—a member of the white, moneyed, mercantile master class of that island. Tituba had also come far, twice removed from her home in West Africa. Indian John, one of whose parents may have been an Indian indigenous to the Caribbean, also found himself in a new and frightening place, dry and hot in summer and icy cold in winter. There they walked dirty, crowded streets among a sea of unfamiliar, pasty faces. Familiar rituals of Afro-Barbadian worship would be replaced, at least in public, by Puritanism. Adaptation to such a world would be difficult.

Unlike the sand spits and gently sloping shores of the Atlantic coastline from Florida to Cape Cod, the New England shore from Boston north to the Canadian Maritimes is rocky, with a few sheltered inlets and harbors, the latter often little more than grassy marshland. To these hard, cold shores had come the first wave of Puritan migrants. Salem was the first of their towns, laid out in 1629. Boston was settled the next year, on a peninsula the Indians called Shawmut. By the 1680s Boston was no longer a frontier village but a commercial center of great activity. In it were about one thousand houses and six thousand people, living on three hills connected to the mainland by a neck of land. Down King Street from the First Church one could find the countinghouses and the wharves, connecting Boston to its lifelines—the coastal, West Indian, and Atlantic trades. Boston was tied to the Atlantic world just as Barbados was, by bonds as strong as the wood of her ships' masts and as frail as the paper used for bills of sale.

Most Bostonians lived in small dwellings on narrow streets, perpetually in shade. Few of these houses had more than a window or two because glass was so expensive and candles were precious. The kitchen was the only warm room in the winter, and no room was cool in the summer. Water had to be doled out, and lumber for building and wood for fuel were costly. Open sewers and rickety outhouses left a permanent miasma in the air, and food soon spoiled if it was not cooked, smoked, or salted. If one could avoid the pox and other epidemic diseases, there were always Indian raids and foreign wars to fear. The inhabitants worked hard, prayed to find in themselves signs of God's grace, and worried about the future.

In Boston Parris married Elizabeth Eldridge, an older woman. They had a son, John, who died in his teens after the witchcraft episode was over and never took part in it; a daughter Elizabeth, called Betty, born in 1683; and another daughter, Susannah, born in 1688. Parris also took charge of his niece, Abigail Williams. He rented a shop and borrowed from family and friends to begin trade once again. A year later he was bogged down in lawsuits for his unpaid bills. Fighting these off made him suspicious of law and wary of trade, although he was still moderately successful. Nevertheless, he knew that he could not rival some of his near neighbors, and this may have galled him because he had experienced exactly the same disparity between aspiration and achievement in Bridgetown.

Sometime in the mid-1680s, Parris began to explore a career in the ministry, for which he had trained during his stint as an undergraduate at Harvard College. His father had been an avid churchgoer and a strong supporter of Puritanism, and his older brother was a minister in England. Samuel had already become a member of the First Church of Boston, sponsored by his minister, James Moody. Parris did not have the academic attainments to compete for the better pulpits, but ministers were always in demand in frontier villages and hamlets. He tried his hand as a guest minister, preaching in Stow in the summer of 1685; when that relationship wilted, he gave talks to private groups and waited for another opportunity.

Parris's heart led him to the ministry. Puritans sought a direct contractual relationship with God that they called a covenant. Perhaps his piety and sense of purpose were strengthened by the preaching he heard when he attended church in Boston. For many Puritans, hearing the preaching of the word was an exhilarating experience. In later days, when he had a pulpit, Parris put much time into writing his sermons. The great Puritan preachers, and there were many in Parris's time, raised the sermon to an art form, the measure and symbol of a culture. Parris worked hard to duplicate their feats.

The church committee from Salem Village had obtained Parris's name. It may be that residents who had had dealings in Barbados recalled him when he began to preach in Stow. Or they may have met him in Boston. First the elders, led by Captain John Putnam Sr., one of the patriarchs of the Village and a selectman for the town, and then a committee of younger men sought him out and invited him to preach in the Village. Parris came in the spring of 1688 and returned in the fall. From November 15, 1688, through April 1689, committees of young and old men from the Village courted Parris. He listened, and finally consented.

Negotiations with the Salem Village deputation took on the characteristics of a business deal, for Parris wanted his new parishioners to bind themselves to support him. The terms of the agreement included a salary of sixty pounds a year, part in money, part in kind, and "when money be more plenteous, the money part to be paid me shall accordingly be increased"; fixed price on the in-kind part of his salary, a hedge against inflation in the price of corn and other provisions; contributions and fees from outside the Village not to count against his income; his own choice of the provisions to be given him as part of his remuneration, so that no one could simply dump surplus or spoilage on him; free firewood (or six pounds more to buy it, later rescinded by consent); two men chosen each year as special collectors to ensure that he was fully paid; and an escalator clause for salary raises "as God shall please to bless this place" with prosperity. Parris's business sense had not deserted him.

Parris's family and servants traveled with him to Salem in September 1689. Within this small circle, he was master. English law and custom gave to the husband the right to dispose of property, discipline wife and children (within reason), and represent the family in the outside world. The relationship he had with his wife cannot be traced, for she is a shadowy figure in all the records, but husband and wife were to love and honor each other. They were not equals—such a thought defied Scripture and reality, and they had different roles to play in the household—but they were to be sturdy mates and fellow travelers on the path of right living. When Elizabeth Parris died, Samuel extolled her as "Best Wife, Choice Mother, Neighbor, Friend."

Puritan parents spent time and effort on their children, and Puritan literature abounds with imaginative concern for the well-being of little ones. One may suspect, from the tenor of his later sermons, that Samuel Parris was a caring, intrusive, moralistic father of a sort then common. As he later told his congregation, the church must be "watchful of sin, even as parents, seeking their young children over bold with Fire, or water, they bring their children neer to the fire, and hold them over the water, as if they would burn them, or drown them whereas they intend nothing less, only to awe them and fright them, that they may hereafter keep farther off."

Far more important for the Parris girls, Betty and Susannah, was their relationship with their mother, about which the records are almost entirely silent. For girls the maternal bond is more important than the paternal one. If little evidence survives of what mothers taught daughters and mistresses imparted to their serving girls, clues to the strength of the bonding marked the pages of mothers' diaries and daughters' letters. Betty probably had a far stronger and more complex relationship with her mother than with her father. The mother-daughter bond constrains and liberates, chafes and nurtures. Girls talk, work, fight, and cry with their mothers. With some exceptions (like witches, who were always assumed to be bad mothers), Puritan mothers loved their children and lamented bitterly their passing. Ann Bradstreet's elegy for a dying grandchild still moves the reader to tears: "[N]o sooner come, but gone, and fal'n asleep, / Acquaintance short, yet parting caus'd us weep.... Go pretty babe, go rest with Sisters twain / Among the blest in endless joyes remain." Mothers cared for children through illness and health, and girls emulated their mothers.

Parris's road to Salem was hardly straight and narrow, but he had chosen the way himself. Tituba and Indian John came as well, for they were slaves and had no choice. They must have comforted each other, both strangers in this strange land, but soon their paths would divide. Tituba remained a house servant, but Parris, still the merchant, would hire Indian John out to work. There were a handful of other black people in the place to which Parris traveled; some had come directly from Africa, others from the West Indies. Some were house servants, like Ann and Candy. Others worked in shops and fields, like Wonn, Tony, and Hager. Some had spouses, like Daniel and Judith. They were not supposed to congregate at taverns after hours, as the white servants did, but some of the male slaves could be found drinking or playing games of chance alongside other working people. Isolated, Tituba was drawn toward the children, and they to her.

Tituba and Parris were much traveled. Both were used to sea travel and may have made the journey from Boston to Salem town, some thirty miles, by coaster. The Salem Village committee had put up the money to bring Parris's predecessor, Deodat Lawson, by boat from Boston to Salem. Salem's seaport was not much different from Boston—a port of entry into the hinterland for the products of the world; a place of debarkation for the produce of the woods, fields, and gardens of New England. On Salem's wharves squealing pigs and stolid cattle milled about as sweating seamen rolled barrels up gangways into the holds of ships. Into the oceangoing ships the dockmen hauled bushels of peas, corn, and oats, and barrels of turnips and Indian squash. Onion was much prized in West Africa; apples and pears were welcomed in the West Indian islands like Jamaica. Fish caught off the shore and in the shallows were salted and packed in the holds as well.

Salem was prosperous, busy, and confident, but the wealth of the few was built upon the poverty of the many. Parris could see the ramshackle shanties of the laborers, cartmen, and fishermen sprawling from the wharves up to the banks of the North River a quarter of a mile distant. Families of sailors and fishermen were crammed into one- and two-room apartments filled with old, rickety furniture and worn wooden eating utensils. Parris, who knew the extremes of wealth and poverty from Barbados and Boston, must have realized that Salem was no exception to the rule that commerce was not a great leveler of fortunes.

From Turner's Wharf on the South River or perhaps another farther along the curve of the harbor, Parris traveled through the town. The houses along the high street were impressive, two and sometimes three stories high, heavy timbered, with red-, yellow-, or green-painted clapboard siding and cedar shingles, overhanging upper floors, dormers, and gables, and a multitude of small, diamond-latticed windows. Parris left Salem along the road to Lynn. Behind him he could see the port; ahead were "the farms"—the original name given Salem Village. The Village's center was four miles before him. All along this part of his route lay the salt marshes; at Trask's Mill they became freshwater marshes, an estuary where the Frost-Fish, the Endicot, and the Bass Rivers all emptied into the bay. Marsh grass had supported the first cattle of the town and still succored extensive herds.

Everywhere the Parris family looked, people worked hard—labor-intensive agriculture in the lands to the west kept Salem's port fed. Farmers' houses lined the road west, their fields a patchwork stretching back from the lanes. As Parris followed the road past Phillips's tavern, he left behind the river traffic and the shops and followed narrower, less crowded ways. The pine clapboard of the farmhouses was no longer painted but weathered, for paint was too expensive and perhaps too gaudy for some of the denizens' tastes. The distance between farmhouses grew. Along the road were fences of timbered wood or stone gathered from the fields. The boulders and stones were a relic of the glaciers, marking the retreat of the wall of ice. Other fences were fashioned from split rails. Parris had traveled a road like this before, when he went to Stow, and he knew that the western edge of the Puritan world was different from its center. But Salem Village would be his home. In this light, the stiffness of his demands during the negotiations became clear—he wanted guarantees that life in his new home would be bearable.

The farmers must have known that Parris and his family were coming, and some no doubt waited by the road to greet him as he passed.

The hellos were more leisurely than in Boston, but the expectations were higher, for in the country the minister was a man of great importance. He was teacher, counselor, consoler, and preacher of God's word. Most of the population of Salem Village, perhaps five hundred souls altogether, congregated in the center of the Village, perhaps by the training ground, or at Nathaniel Ingersoll's tavern that stood at the crossing of the road from Salem and Meetinghouse Lane, to greet the new preacher and his family.

Parris saw immediately that the singing of psalms and the raucous shouts of the drunken shuffleboard players would mingle in the air at that corner of the Village, for he would teach and preach in the shadow of the tavern. Public drunkenness was a misdemeanor in law and was prosecuted at the quarterly sessions of the peace, but that was no balm to Parris or his more pious and respectable parishioners. When the tipplers spilled out onto the porch of the tavern, the quarrels and curses of the drinkers could be heard in the parsonage and the meetinghouse. When they got excited, defamers called down the Devil Himself upon their adversaries or accused one who offended of being an "old witch, old wizard." Parris was no innocent, however; from his days in Barbados he knew what sin looked and smelled like.

If the tavern marked the irrepressibility of the profane, the parsonage and the meetinghouse symbolized the physical and spiritual center of the community. Standing just off the crossing of the two major roads in the Village, they gave the cluster of homes and shops its collective identity. Parris and his family were to live in the parsonage built in 1681 for George Burroughs, one of Parris's predecessors, and later occupied by Deodat Lawson, Parris's immediate precursor. The house was a two-story clapboard with a central chimney and four fireplaces, surrounded by two acres of meadowland; a path across part of the meadow took Parris to the meetinghouse without having to walk past the tavern.

The meetinghouse stood on a small rise, facing the road. Completed over a five-year span between 1672 and 1677, it was an unimposing building, resembling more than anything else a large farmhouse. Boxlike in shape, twenty-seven by thirty-six by twenty-eight feet high, with two windows on each side and a small entry porch in the front, it was already in need of repair after fifteen years of New England winters and summers. The windows were small, latticed with diamond-shaped glass. Little light came through them but that was not important, for light was supposed to come from the pulpit. The house of God was an auditory, a place to listen, its interior designed so that everyone who came faced the preacher and could hear his words. Nothing was to detract from God's word. The congregation seated itself according to age and economic status, the best people in the front pews. Children sat with their parents or on the stairs. Servants and slaves were welcome, but they sat in the back.

Parris gave his ordination sermon in that meetinghouse. For the Puritan minister and his congregation, the sermon was a crucial part of the worship service. In it the minister became the Lord's messenger. The sermon preached by a minister at his ordination was the most important sermon of all, for at this service the ministry itself was reconsecrated, the covenant of the minister and his flock with God was renewed, and the godly community was reestablished. To Parris's ordination sermon came Nicholas Noyes, the assistant pastor of Salem's church; John Hale from Beverly; and Samuel Phillips from Rowley. Phillips, the oldest at sixty-three, laid on the right hand of fellowship, "with beautiful loveliness and humility."

Public preaching in the house of worship brought minister and flock together. The sermon demonstrated the minister's familiarity with Christian teachings and reached out to the hearts of the worshipers. With them, as Parris wrote in the church records for that day, he began a conversation in piety and mutual love.

> We whose names . . . are hereunto subscribed, lamenting our great unfitness [for such] an awful and solemn approach unto the Holy God and [deploring] all the miscarriages committed by us, either in the days [of] our unregeneracy or since we have been brought into acquaintance with God in the communion of his churches . . . yet apprehending ourselves called by the Most High to embody [ourselves] into a different society . . . this day give up ourselves one unto another in the Lord.

Ingersoll signed, as did Nathaniel and John Putnam Sr., the committeemen who had brought Parris to the Village. Thomas, John Jr., Edward, Jonathan, and Benjamin Putnam added their names, along with Henry and Benjamin Wilkins and their father, Bray. Others joined. Notably absent were the largest landholders and richest men in the

Village, the Porters, for they were members of John Higginson's church in Salem, but they did come this day to hear the ordination sermon.

For the day Parris had chosen as his text Josh. 5:9: "And the Lord said unto Joshua: This Day I have rolled away the Reproach of Egypt from off you." This was the divine promise for those who were within the covenant. For those who did not subscribe to it, there was only danger, for the Lord warned the Egyptian, the Canaanite, and all rebels from Heaven that they would be rooted out from the earth. Parris thought that this doctrine was "exceedingly useful for our unbelieving days." Too many who should have been members of the church had ignored their religious duties. Sinners, they thought they had time enough, but it was almost too late. Prosperity came to those who walked in the path of piety. Massachusetts was a new Israel, for its people made a covenant with God, just like Abraham's seed, and the prophets of the Old Testament foretold the coming of the Christian Messiah, just as Parris preached the word in the meetinghouse. His congregation stood in Israel's place, but to receive this blessing they had to renew the visible and sacramental communion with God. Then the eyes of the blind would be opened to the joy of God's care; Christ in his majesty would be present in the church.

Parris ended his sermon with a personal message to his congregation: "Much work is laid, or like to be laid, upon my weak shoulders. . . . I am to carry it not as a Lord, but as a servant. . . . I am to labor that my doctrine may burn, and my conversation may shine. . . . As I am to give Cordials to some, so I must be sure to administer corrosives to others." Heavy was Parris's burden; his congregation had to help:

> You are to pay me that Reverence which is due to an Embassadour of Christ Jesus. You are to bear me a great deal of love. . . . You are to obey me (at least) so far as I watch for your souls. . . . You are to pray for me and to pray such and fervently always for me, but especially when you expect to hear from God by me. . . . You are to endeavor by all lawfull means to make my heavy work as much as in you lies light and cheerful . . . and not . . . to make my life among you grievous, and my labor among you unprofitable.

He wanted from his parishioners a contract similar to the one he had negotiated with the Village committee. Such a contract echoed that between God and His chosen people, and Parris referred to the higher covenant by reminding his listeners that he was Christ's emissary on earth. Ministers often manipulated their congregants' desire to gain the minister's approbation in order to reach their hearts and help them seek God, but Parris's requirement went the other way. He demanded that his flock love him. He built this argument upon the likeness between a gathered church and a Puritan family. The minister, he hinted, is the father, to whom the other family members owe obedience. But there was no family—no network of kin, save a distant brother and his family—to supplement his reserves of spiritual strength or reassure him in time of need. Nor was there a connection that time and mutual care had woven with other ministers in his cohort. In Salem he was as isolated in heart as he was in body.

Parris, no less than Tituba (though she more visibly), remained an outsider in the Village. He had traveled far from home, leaving one calling for another to answer the summons of the Villagers. And there was the irony, for in the place where Parris sought peace and fulfillment, neither could be found. In these days Salem was suffering its own trials, which would soon sweep up Parris and his household into a flood of recrimination.

The Village

In 1689 the town of Salem, including Salem Village, was rapidly changing. It had once been a compact settlement of farmers and fishermen. There was trade, but making money through trade did not dominate the thoughts of the townspeople, nor did the merchants command the town government. The farmers and fishermen deferred to a few well-recognized leaders, worshiped together in a single church, and met together for the muster of the militia. It was an honor to hold a town office. By the 1680s that world was passing. Salem's men and women witnessed the rise of a powerful mercantile elite, many of its members newcomers to the town. Outlying areas like Beverly had broken away from Salem and become new towns. More and more often, prominent townspeople refused to serve as local officers.

The Village, a part of the town and isolated in some respects, experienced the pains of transformation but lacked the resources that enabled the more settled wards of the town to cope with change. In Salem as a whole, the shift to commerce and overseas trade could be accommodated, for it went hand in hand with capital accumulation, diversification of investment, and the rise of new and successful types of enterprises. For the Village the same innovations could not be weathered as easily, because the Villagers lacked the capital, labor, and skills to partake of the advantages of the market, and because the rivalry of two families, fostered in part by the economic changes, split the Villagers' allegiances.

Originally, the farms of the Village had been a neighborhood, a group of families starting out more or less even in the quest for land and power. As the land around the Village passed to second and third generations, some families proved more successful than others. What emerged was a hierarchy of families organized by rank. Village marriage patterns reinforced this hierarchy. The fortunate families added to their wealth and status through marriage, the survival of children, and long residence in the area. Over time, kin became clan, and clan loyalty, stretched across generations, became a surrogate for political party in local contests for office. By the time Parris arrived, two clans vied for control of the Village and its pulpit—the Putnams and the Porters.

The Putnams had appeared in Salem in the early 1640s. The patriarch was John Putnam, who emigrated from England to Massachusetts in his sixties. By 1662, at the age of eighty-two, he had amassed over eight hundred acres of land and had three surviving sons, two known locally by their militia ranks, Lieutenant Thomas and Captain John, the other named Nathaniel. To his sons, before he died, the elder Putnam gave land in the far west of the township. They, in turn, bestowed farmland on their children, dividing what had been a substantial holding into smaller and smaller parcels. The Putnam children married into other well-to-do local families, like the Hutchinsons, the Ingersolls, the Sibleys, the Houltons, the Walcotts, and the Buxtons. Hutchinson, Ingersoll, and Houlton owned large lots near the village parsonage. Sibley and Walcott lived even closer to the meetinghouse. Like a ring of outworks around a fortress, farms owned and worked by the third generation of Putnams—Jonathan Putnam, James Putnam, Joseph Putnam, John Putnam Jr. (the son of Captain John)—and Nathaniel Putnam surrounded the church and parsonage.

Lieutenant Thomas Putnam died in 1686, but before he passed away, he prepared a will that further divided his lands among his children. The largest portion went to Joseph Putnam, the only issue of the elder Thomas's son by his second wife, Mary Veren. They got the family farm. Joseph married Elizabeth Porter, daughter of Israel Porter, a far more advantageous marriage than those of Joseph's brothers, for it linked Joseph to the only family whose wealth could rival his own.

The other children had not done quite as well. Sergeant Thomas, Joseph's older half brother, married Ann Carr, daughter of a wealthy family, but acquired nothing of her inheritance, a sore point with him. His brothers and cousins tried their hand at West Indian commerce, ironmongery, and land speculation but were not successful. Politically, they had no better luck. The elder Putnams, like Captain John, served occasionally as selectmen for the town well into the 1680s, but his son John Jr. and other Putnams in his son's generation were unable to retain the family's political influence in the town's council. The younger sons' ambitions fell back upon the Village. The youngsters were litigious as well, often coming to court to defend their interests in land. The Porters first came to Salem in the 1640s, led by John Porter, an English immigrant in his forties. Before his death in 1676, he owned over two thousand acres, in addition to mills, inns, and other properties. According to the first tax census in Salem, completed in 1681, the Porters were richer than the Putnams. Four sons—John, Joseph, Benjamin, and Israel—outlived their father. John and Benjamin never married, but their brothers had large families. Instead of seeking to gain lands in the west, they looked to the east and commerce. Porter children married into the mercantile elite of Salem, including two of the richest men in the county, Daniel Andrew and Thomas Gardiner. As Putnam political fortunes in the town waned, Porter fortunes waxed. By the 1680s, Israel Porter was a perennial member of the town's selectmen, joined occasionally by his brothers-in-law Andrew and Gardiner.

There were plenty of householders who knew the Putnams and Porters well, had dealings with them, but were not affiliated to them by marriage or bonds of loyalty. These included some of the older families like Giles and Martha Corey, George Jacobs Sr. and his children, the Towne sisters—Rebecca Nurse, Sarah Cloyse, and Mary Esty—and the Proctors. Some of the latter, like George Jacobs, had a long history of abusing others, fighting, and getting into trouble with the justices of the peace, while others, like Francis and Rebecca Nurse, were men and women of admirable charity, who took in the orphan and cared for the sick. The Village also had its marginal members, who moved from household to household doing odd jobs, sometimes begging for handouts. Some of these people were young laborers, for whom poverty was just a stage in their life course. For others, like Sarah Good, whose panhandling had become a matter of general irritation, it had become a career.

The Putnams and the Porters were the most visible laypeople in the community, and status brought with it obligation. They were expected to provide political leadership. Their own interests, however, pointed them in opposite directions when it came to matters of policy. That is, rather than speaking for a united Village, they came to speak for factions they themselves led. The crucial test in this growing contest for power was the two families' opposing plans for the future of the Village.

The Putnams worked hard to make the Village independent of the rest of the old town. They tried a direct approach, seeking permission of the selectmen; they tried to get around the opposition of their coastal neighbors by appealing to the General Court; they assayed a nibbling approach, seeking reduction of tax rates. They had some success. The Villagers were legally residents of the town of Salem, but they had gradually loosened the ties that bound them to the older parts of the town. In 1667 many of the homesteaders in the Village petitioned the General Court in Boston for an exemption from the watch duties that every head of family had to fulfill. The men of the Village explained that they lived from five to ten miles from the watch house in Salem, and had to march those miles fully armed, leaving their families prey to Indian raids. Assembling the Village contingent took time, for the houses were dispersed, some a mile away from the center of population and the training ground in the Village, and marching to the town center consumed still more time, while the sickly and weak at home were left unprotected. The Village troops comprised but three dozen, whose coming to the aid of the rest of the watch—three hundred strong—seemed a misallocation of force, given the dangers that the Village faced in those times. A terrible war with the Indians lay but a decade in the future, and the General Court recognized the justice of the Villagers' plea, granting them the exemption from military service in the town center. Three years later, the Villagers again approached the General Court, seeking permission to erect their own meetinghouse and select their own preacher rather than travel the road to Salem on the Sabbath. In 1672 the General Court gave them the right to build a house of worship and to name a committee to gather funds for a minister who would reside among them.

Surely resentment of the increasingly commercial policy of the new generation of the town's leaders entered into their calculations, but the Putnams valued the advantages of commerce, and the Village benefited from the commercial success of the harbor wards. Salem Village was still overwhelmingly agricultural, but its men and women went to town often enough, and the Putnams had no desire to sever themselves from trade with the port. The Putnams differed from the leaders of the old town not because commerce flourished along the coast and faltered in the Village but because they, like most of the Villagers, looked to the interior of the colony, a vast space potentially filled with family farms. To fully associate themselves with this farming interest, the Putnams reasoned that they must have political autonomy from the seaport.

The Porters, for reasons of their own, stood in the way, for complete independence for the Village would put the Porters (who, after all, lived in the Village) at the mercy of the Putnams. The Porters did not withdraw their interest in Village affairs but instead quietly interfered with the Putnams' plans for the Village's independence. The Porters' answer to the Putnams' efforts was to fashion closer ties to the rest of the town, based on participation in the world market. Most of the well-to-do farmers of eastern Massachusetts were already selling some portion of their produce to distant markets and buying the products of the Atlantic trade, but they still thought in local terms. Not so the Porters. Their ambitions stretched to more distant horizons. The Porters had married into mercantile families whose interests reached across the Atlantic to the British Isles and from West Africa to the Caribbean. Perhaps this was a truer vision of the future than the Putnams', for such commerce would bring great wealth to the merchants of Salem in the next century.

As the two families began to develop a network of alliances based on marriage, disputes over land surveys and unpaid debts became tests of clan loyalty. When these disputes came into the local courts, clan leaders looked to these alliances for support. For example, when Nathaniel Putnam claimed that a piece of his land was wrongly occupied by another—and he did this all the time—to his support came his in-laws, his married and unmarried children, and his friends. In the 1670s and 1680s, such private civil suits for unpaid debts and unfulfilled obligations merged and overlapped as the Putnams' personal quarrels became Village-wide controversies.

The Putnams were not averse to taking matters into their own hands when they became impatient, sometimes cutting down trees and carting away the timber on other people's farms. They turned to the courts, however, to resolve a long-standing dispute with the town of Topsfield, over whose border some of Nathaniel Putnam's lands supposedly lay. To determine how much Putnam could claim, Topsfield appointed Jacob Townes and John Howe to approach Captain John Putnam and "any other" Salem men and ask for the legal deeds, but the Putnams could not produce documentary evidence. They testified instead that the lands were given them by the General Court. Appealed to by the Topsfield men, the General Court tried to quiet the dispute over title to the lands, but the feud continued even after the lands were resurveyed.

By the 1680s the conflict between the Putnams and the Hobbs-Esty-Howe-Towne-Wildes families of Topsfield was an ominous fact of Village life. In January 1687 the dispute took a new direction, for the Howes had gained allies in the Village. Joseph Porter and his brother-in-law Daniel Andrew joined Topsfield's Isaac Esty as witnesses that Captain John Putnam had felled timber on land that, according to Howe, did not belong to any Putnam. The Putnams retorted by convincing a Salem grand jury to present Esty for "telling a lie in open court." The dispute over timber and meadow refused to die, for out-of-court animosities ran deep. Some of these must have spilled over into the way the Putnams regarded the Topsfield women who lived in the Village—Rebecca Nurse, Mary Esty, and Sarah Cloyse.

The ministry inevitably became another focal point of these tensions, as a succession of ministers quarreled with important members of the leading clans, who, their dignity offended, insisted that the minister be dismissed. To the minister's defense in turn came other factions within the clan structure, in the process of which personal disagreements became public disputes. Having received, after five years of agitation, permission from the General Court to build their own meetinghouse and hire their own preacher, the freeholders of Salem Village engaged James Bayley to be their religious leader on November 11, 1672. A young graduate of Harvard College, Bayley was not an ordained minister, but the Village committee gave him a salary of forty pounds to lead services. The next year the Villagers asked Bayley to remain, but by 1679 he had done something to offend Bray Wilkins, a substantial farmer and close friend of Nathaniel Putnam and John Jr. For his own part, Bayley had friends in the Putnam clan, notably Lieutenant Thomas Putnam and his son Sergeant Thomas, and Captain John Putnam. When a petition against the pastor came to their hands, they retorted that Bayley had been chosen "by the great consent and vote of the inhabitants." Bayley's supporters insisted that outside authority be called to arbitrate the dispute, and their brothers and cousins and friends agreed. John Higginson, Salem's venerable pastor, investigated and reported that Bayley had done no wrong. Bayley still wanted the job, and the Villagers met and voted to retain him for the next year. Now Nathaniel and John Jr. swung into action, rallying support for an appeal to the General Court. The upper house of the General Court supported the Higginson report, but the lower house agreed with the Village meeting. Bayley stayed for his year, then left.

Bayley's case did not pit Putnams against Porters, but it did demonstrate that personal slights could become public issues when the local magnates felt they had been offended. As Bayley's case proved, the Putnams might not always agree among themselves, but when they did, they could control the nomination of ministers. They chose as Bayley's replacement George Burroughs. Burroughs had graduated from Harvard a year after Bayley, in 1670, and had preached in Falmouth, Maine, on Casco Bay, until the Indian uprising called King Philip's War (1675–76) devastated the area. With other Maine settlers, Burroughs relocated to Massachusetts, where the committee found him and offered him the Village pulpit. He arrived in 1681 to the newly built parsonage and the same salary of sixty pounds that Bayley had received in his terminal year—and something of the same troubles.

Burroughs's wife soon died, and he had to borrow money to pay for the customary funeral wine. Captain John Putnam was happy to help, but within a year dissension divided the two men. "Brother against brother and neighbor against neighbor" was how Jeremiah Watts put it on April 11, 1682. Watts was accurate: the brothers were again the elder Putnams. The Village committee was indeed unhappy with its selection. Most unhappy was Captain John, who had lent Burroughs money a year before but now held up the minister's salary. When Lieutenant Thomas hesitated about harassing Burroughs, Captain John grabbed his brother by the coat and changed his mind. Burroughs had offended Captain John by refusing to preach unless he was paid and by planning openly to leave. Captain John, joined by Lieutenant Thomas and Nathaniel, first petitioned the court to force Burroughs to stay, the latter supposedly having committed himself to live among them and preach. When this failed, Captain John filed suit for the debt. When Burroughs appeared in the village to settle his accounts, Putnam arranged for the town marshal to seize the minister. Nathaniel Putnam, with Ingersoll and Sibley, put up the bail—perhaps still hoping that Burroughs would change his mind. Burroughs had no sooner answered their charges than the Putnams withdrew the suit—Captain John's honor satisfied and the power of his family to appoint and dispose confirmed.

Burroughs left, and Deodat Lawson of Norfolk, England, arrived. He came to Massachusetts in the 1670s and floundered around for a time until he was called to the Village pulpit. In 1686 his Putnam supporters, seeking leverage in their effort to make the town and its church independent of Salem, pressed for his ordination. Captain John and his son John Jr. led the effort, but by now a new group had emerged to challenge the Putnams' hitherto unshakable control of the meetinghouse. Led by Joseph Putnam and Daniel Andrew, the dissenters wanted a full discussion. Again the Village had to ask for outside help, this time from a committee from the seaport, including merchants Bartholomew Gedney, John Hathorne, and William Brown Jr., only to discover that the mediators advised against ordination of Lawson. He left shortly thereafter. Behind the opposition to Lawson stood the Porters. By now, Village factionalism had become notorious in eastern Massachusetts.

Samuel Parris's appointment fell into this widening crevasse. The Putnams chose him, and over time anti-Putnam men became his opponents. The clear lines of pro- and anti-Parris affiliation did not come until the witchcraft crisis was under way, however. Thus it was not a clash of clans that made Parris's life so hard in the Village; it was Parris himself. Unlike his three predecessors, who in varying ways would have preferred to avoid controversy, he sided with those who supported him and preached against those who refused to contribute to the upkeep of the church and to seek full membership in it. The anti-Parris faction retaliated at a Village meeting on October 16, 1691, when the Putnam-dominated rate committee was ousted and Joseph Porter, Joseph Hutchinson, Joseph Putnam (who had cast his lot with his wife's family, the Porters), Daniel Andrew, and Francis Nurse were chosen in their stead. Parris replied by summoning his supporters to a meeting in the parsonage and pleading for their aid. The breach widened but was yet bridgeable, for Nurse, Hutchinson, Porter, Nathaniel Putnam, and John Jr. that same week joined in an appeal to the town council to reduce the Village's rates.

Who was to resolve differences like these when they mirrored the social antagonisms and the political rivalry of the leading families? The Village lacked a regular town government. The householders met and selected a committee whose decisions were binding on those who were willing to be bound, but appeals lay to the town and to the courts. All the towns in the colony were the creatures of the General Court, the legislature of the colony, and in past years the Village had gained relief from the General Court. But the General Court came into being under the old charter of 1629, and the Crown had abrogated that charter in 1684. A Dominion of New England had replaced the old government, but most of the settlers suspected the motives of its leaders. No one could be certain what the future held for the towns or for the colony.

In 1689 the politics of the colony passed from uncertainty to uproar. Learning that the hated King James II had been driven from his throne, a party of merchants and ministers thrust Governor Edmund Andros, Dudley's replacement, from his post and imprisoned him. A provisional government was hastily erected. There were still courts—the Court of Assistants met, as did the local courts—and they maintained to some extent the sense of community that the fathers of the towns wanted. Nevertheless, Provisional Governor Simon Bradstreet was old and tired; his councillors (many of the same men who had served Andros's Dominion, and, before him, the first charter government) were uneasy. Left to themselves, the Villagers had turned the selection of a new minister into a purely factional issue. Porter dissent prevented the Putnams from exercising their authority and Parris from gaining the security he needed.

In these times of troubles, ministers reassured their congregants. Now more than ever, Parris's role in the community should have gone beyond formal pastoral and ministerial tasks, to make sense of a world coming apart. Uncertainty about colonial politics had reinforced the importance of traditional forms of information gathering. Simple words of comfort would outweigh whole libraries of learned tracts. In this the minister had a special role to play. Parris preached twice on the Lord's day, and perhaps once during the week, in addition to leading lessons and counseling privately. He was the arbiter of disputes and the source of information, and the congregation should have been eager for his ministrations.

In the face of growing local factionalism and colonywide disorder, Parris remained outwardly calm, though one can almost hear the crackling of the discipline in his voice. On November 22, 1691, he began a series of lectures on the text of Psalm 110: "The Lord said unto my Lord, sit thou at my right hand until I make thine enemies thy footstool." The first two lectures, delivered that day, traced the importance of Christ's ascension and His place at the right hand of the Father. Consolation was Parris's theme and his purpose. The psalm "is made up of many pretious promises, that have a direct tendency to the consolation of the Faithful." Parris had opened the door a crack to his yearning congregation, allowing them to see Christ, wounded and humiliated, rise again. Parris was sending the message that those who sought the Lord would be saved. Christ interceded and mediated for the sinner. He came before the Father and pleaded with all His sufferings as tokens of His earnestness, that "[t]he worth of souls is above all the world."

These words of comfort came not from Christ, of course, but from His servant Samuel Parris. As he told his congregants in the second two lectures, given on the morning and afternoon of January 3, the role of the minister was essential in the gathered church. From within the flock of saints He gathered, Christ chose a few to preach the word, and "for this purpose Christ hath given ministers" to his people, "by which means the dark minds of the Elect are enlightened and their hard hearts are softened." But even the elect must pay attention to the preaching of the minister, Parris reminded the stiff-necked in his congregation, for opposition to him was opposition to the Word. They, too, should fear the wiles of Satan, for proud hearts that resisted the ministrations of the preacher could not be open to God's grace. Nevertheless, Parris held out an open hand to those who would return to the faith of their fathers.

The Parris who read these sermons was a man striving to rise above his troubles. Because of his background, he had faced obstacles that others in his situation had not. He had not grown to manhood in New England, nor did he have intimate contact with the ministry there. His relative inexperience with the ways of the men and women of the farming interior had left him impatient with his parishioners and insensitive to their expectations. He was no provincial, whatever they might be, but a man of the Atlantic world, and some of his parishioners did not understand the sacrifice he had made to live among them. Nevertheless, Parris still walked the high road, disciplining the arrogance bred in the scions of the plantation master class. Bereft of parents and kin, without long-term friends, newly installed in a calling whose other professors were well established and more experienced than he, he coped. Caught in a long-standing feud between powerful political factions, he wanted to minister to the souls of all and hoped for a day when all would present themselves for full membership in the church. Parris resented the failure of the new Village committee to pay what they owed him, but he could contain that resentment so long as his pastoral duties went well.

This was the winter of his third year in Salem. Sixty-one people had joined the church, which was gratifying, but only one member came forward to seek full communion. In orthodox fashion, Parris insisted that the Lord's Supper was not meant to bring a person to grace—instead, it was reserved for those who had been chosen and could demonstrate to the congregation that they were ready for full membership. So, too, under Parris's leadership, the congregation still rejected the more liberal implications of the "half-way covenant," allowing the children of churchgoers to participate in communion, though they had no personal experience of grace to relate. Parris worried that many who were regenerate simply did not believe in themselves, and he begged them to come forward and join their fellows. He would not credit the idea that he was the cause of the decline in church membership, but he worried aloud that a malignity was abroad, some evil force that had crept into the meetinghouse and spread its wings of doubt and backbiting among his parishioners.

Early in January, after Parris preached his sermons on the intercessory care of Christ, a crisis of faith erupted in the Village that made the division of the congregation unmistakably clear. Despite an opinion on the matter of his salary from the Essex County Quarterly Court delivered on January 17, 1692, ordering the Village committee, still dominated by Parris's enemies, to meet and collect funds for Parris's salary, the committee dithered. That rankled but did not surprise Parris, given the committee's prior position. If the records show no single episode that broke his will, the strokes of misfortune continued to fall. He had offered conciliation in the bosom of Chirst and his opponents returned ill will and contumely. His supporters, particularly the Putnams, had other reasons to dislike and distrust Parris's assailants in the Village and probably stoked Parris's frustration and anger.

The pattern of his earlier failures seemed to be repeating itself. He decided to strike back at his, and God's, enemies.

Parris finished his lecture series on the ascension of Christ on February 14, but the tone of this final sermon was entirely different from that of the previous four. Instead of proving that men and women had a friend sitting at the right hand of the Father, Parris warned that Christ's ascension put one more judge of iniquity into the heavens. Parris thundered: "It is a woeful piece of our corruption in an evil time, when the wicked prosper and the godly party meet with vexations." Now there was a godly party, beset with troubles: yes, "and now we call the proud happy: yea, they that work wickedness are set up." Parris no longer consoled or sought unity. Instead, he condemned—and through him, Christ condemned—those who refused to help Parris do God's work. The reference to the proud and the "set up" referred to the committee elected by the Village. Parris sent an unmistakable message to Israel and Joseph Porter and their allies: "[B]ecause stronger is he that is with us and for us, than he that is against us," they would pay, in the next world if not in this, for their iniquities. Christ, no longer the gentle mediator who pleaded with His own suffering for the salvation of souls, became the judge and the executioner. Ministers in His service were to "endeavor a true separation between the precious and the vile, and to labour what in them lyes to gather a pure Church unto Christ. . . . others we are to refuse and reject."

In Salem that winter, Parris finally joined wholeheartedly in the partisan backbiting. Menace and ill will floated on the chill, damp air. Danger reared up in his own meetinghouse and on the paths from the parsonage to the Village center. Undistracted, Parris might have stayed above it, but he believed himself besieged by enemies, and the evil crept into his own home.

Then there was the cold. Winter was a hard time for ministers and their congregants, for New England winters are severe, but this was worse. Climatologists have found that the 1690s marked a "little ice age" throughout North America. Even in the meetinghouse, the bitter cold crept through the walls and under the doors, reaching Parris in his raised pulpit. He wore a heavy gown and gloves; his parishioners bundled up; but there was no heat (there was no fireplace in the meetinghouse), and Parris had to break off his preaching "by reason of the

Cold." The fields were frozen, and to go out one had to dress warmly in cloth and wool, or fur, if one could afford it and was permitted to wear it. To go indoors one had to bundle up as well, for the only source of heat was the fireplace, and fireplaces in wooden homes were not efficient sources of heat. Night came early, and with it, more cold. Without a ready supply of firewood, another of Parris's complaints, the parsonage was nearly as cold as the meetinghouse. Parris carped that his house was cold. The cold sifted through the rooms and into his family's spirits.

The worsening weather brought sore throats, fevers, and hacking coughs that could be heard throughout houses and passed from Villager to Villager. Refugees from the Indian raids to the north and west brought with them additional sicknesses. Infirmity was common, but in Salem one child became especially and strangely ill: Betty in the Parris household. Elizabeth Parris Sr., her hands full with little Susannah, tried to cope, but Betty's ailment resisted all remedy. Whispers that Betty's illness was not natural soon traveled through the Village, mingling with the rumors of death and destruction on the frontier. Surely the Devil was near.

CHAPTER 3

Witchcraft Suspected

Serious illness was not uncommon among the young in this world; a New England mother and father could expect more than one of their children to die before reaching adulthood. But Betty Parris was not merely sick in bed. She dashed about, lashed out, and dove under furniture. Her cousin Abigail followed suit. The parsonage echoed with strange shrieks as the winter grew colder and the girls got sicker. Soon, other girls who had visited and played with Betty began to complain of similar symptoms. Eleven-year-old Ann Putnam Jr., whose father, Sargeant Thomas, and uncle Captain John were Parris's great supporters in his troubles, and Mercy Lewis, a servant in the Thomas Putnam household, were beset, as was Mary Walcott, who lived next door to the parsonage. The circle of contagion spread to other girls, including the Village doctor's niece, Elizabeth Hubbard.

No one will ever know what really caused Betty's travail. The case may have been partly psychological. Scholars have speculated that Betty and the other girls became hysterical or that the girls were possessed. Similar episodes of possession documented by contemporaries in early modern Europe also involved girls or young women. Modern doctors who have examined the records have offered various diagnoses. One scholar has offered asthma as a possible culprit. In many of these conditions, whether asthma, epilepsy, or some form of acute delusional psychosis, situational stress can bring on illness.

The girls undoubtedly knew about Samuel Parris's troubles. In the parsonage the children's bedroom on the second floor stood directly above the first-floor parlor, a large room where Parris met his parishioners. The floorboards of the upper rooms were single planks, filled with knotholes and badly joined. Through the cracks sand and dirt fell to the floor below, and sounds traveled upward. One can see Betty and

Abigail with their ears or eyes pressed to the cracks as Parris and his supporters rehearsed the travails of his ministry in the parlor below.

Every morning, as the family studied together, working its way through the two Testaments, Parris prayed with Betty for her recovery. He also used the occasion to remind her that she should prepare herself for God's judgment. Fear drove Parris—fear for Betty, fear for the efficacy of his prayers, and fear for the unregenerate, whom, he believed, prayed in vain. Yet prayer brought no cure, for Betty's sufferings continued.

A good parent not only prayed with a child but also provided an example of grace and perseverance in hard times. Unfortunately, Parris's temper was frayed, and his family devotions must have crackled with the strain, just as his sermons showed his anger. Such prayers were more than supplications; they were confessions of human error as well. When Parris prayed, he was expected to admit his own sins. In beseeching divine assistance, Parris had to confess error. It must have occurred to him that some of his troubles were his own fault, the result of his stiff-necked, demanding personality. A ministry that was supposed to rest upon the love between the minister and his flock had turned hateful. The pain of his failed expectations reverberated in his daughter's complaints.

Thus far there were no witches in Salem, only sick girls, worried mothers, and fathers with strong wills. Parris's quarrel with some of his parishioners was not unusual in New England towns, but the shadow of witchcraft was not far away. It lurked in the very midst of a popular culture of spirits and omens that Parris and his parishioners shared. Everyone believed in the existence of the Devil, that the Devil made pacts with witches, and that witches' spells, curses, and evil eyes could harm the innocent and the godly.

Parris finally consulted William Griggs, a new doctor in the neighborhood allied to the Putnams by marriage, and Griggs decided that Betty's illness was not natural. Unlike the ministers, who counseled each other to be cautious, Dr. Griggs preferred a supernatural explanation. Rumor had it that Griggs had used this diagnosis before, but he was not the only physician in Essex County to conclude, when his own nostrums failed, that his patient was bewitched. After Elizabeth Kelley, the nine-year-old daughter of John Kelley of Hartford, Connecticut, died in 1662 under suspicious circumstances, Dr. Bryan

Rosseter deposed that the cause of death defied medical knowledge. In a deposition against Mary Bradbury, James Carr reported that some twenty years before a Dr. Crosbe had treated Carr for fits with "visek" (physic) soaked in tobacco; when that failed, Crosbe told Carr that he was "behaged."

It was common knowledge that witches targeted children. Well over half the indictments against witches in England involved the sickness or death of children. Popular books on witchcraft described how witches used "oil of live infants stolen out of the cradle or dead ones stolen out of their graves" to make a magical unguent or jelly. Acquitted of charges of witchcraft in 1651, Mary Parsons of Springfield, Massachusetts, acknowledged that she was guilty of infanticide. Her own child, sick and wasting, had died by her hand. Neighbors suspected her of bewitching the child, but her act, confessed at last, was not supernatural at all. Nevertheless, when the tale was retold in popular imagination (and later written down by John Hale), it became a proof that the Devil hungered for the souls of the despairing mother so much that He took the form of the dying child to tempt Goody Parsons. The death of otherwise healthy babies was attributed to Bridget Bishop, the first Salem witch to be executed. Fourteen years before the Salem crisis erupted, Bishop was seen in the rooms of infants at night, and soon afterward the infants sickened and died.

Parris was not yet convinced, but Betty and Abigail grew worse. Almost beside himself with worry, Parris nevertheless listened to his brethren in the ministry, prayed, and waited for some sign. If he had read William Perkins, Puritanism's foremost authority on witchcraft, Parris would have learned that witches could indeed hurt the innocent, and even the godly were not immune. Other Puritan writers like John Bernard and John Gaule agreed that everyone was at risk, but the faithful must put their trust in their Maker. Boston minister Increase Mather, who reported cases of such affliction in Massachusetts, agreed that the only cure came from prayer, faith, and seeking protection within the covenant with God. On the scene, Hale told Parris to put his faith in God.

Others were not so patient. Betty's illness had become public knowledge and was read as a sign that greater evils loomed ahead. While Parris fretted and consulted ministers and doctors—members of a professional, elite culture—his near neighbor, Mary Sibley, the mother of another afflicted girl, Mary Walcott, delved into the folklore of countermagic and acted. The Sibleys lived at the foot of Thorndike Hill, not a quarter mile from the parsonage. Mary Sibley was related by marriage to the Putnams and had been admitted to membership in the Salem Village church under the guidance of Parris in 1690. She knew that neighbors had an obligation to assist one another in time of trouble, particularly when a child's health was at stake. With her neighbors' sickness unabated by the ministrations of concerned clergy and doctors, Sibley proposed an old English folk remedy to find the unnatural source of Betty's illness that Griggs had diagnosed. Sibley asked Tituba and Indian John to bake a rye cake with the urine of the victims and feed it to a hound, supposedly a "familiar" of the witch, an intermediary sent by the Devil to carry out the witches' commands. Taking urine from supposed victims of witchcraft was a common practice in countermagic.

Sibley had crossed a line between being a good neighbor and practicing as a "cunning woman," a folk doctor, a crossing that brought her uncomfortably close to being a witch, but it was a line over which New Englanders regularly stepped. In times of stress, formal religion, with its priests and books of prayers, may not comfort so much as older customs. The Puritans were not above calling upon folkways, or rather, because Puritanism overlay a set of folkways, Puritans could always turn to traditions of managing life, illness, and death other than those precepts taught by their ministers.

The line between orthodoxy and folk religion could be blurred by the way in which "regular" medicine was practiced. Griggs's predecessor in Salem, Dr. Zerobabel Endecott, had in his notebooks a regimen for distraction "in a woman" that rivaled Sibley's recipe: "Tak milk of a Nurce that gives such to a male Child and alse take a hee Catt and cut of one of his Ears or a peece of it and lett it blede into the milk and then lett the sick woman drink it. Do this three times." The prescription might work or not—for contemporaries the important consideration was that this remedy was perfectly normal. In this context, the ingredients of the witch cake were not drastically different from orthodox medical treatment.

Sibley knew who were the supposed victims of witches. In the main, they were men and women who had wronged the very people they would later accuse of witchcraft. When the accusers fell ill or lost wealth, or faced other events they could not explain, they remembered who they had maltreated. And who in reality—not in fevered imagination or angry denunciation—were the accused? Very often they were men and women with long histories of being accused of something or other—in effect "the usual suspects." They most often lived literally and figuratively on the margins of communities. Outcasts without being thrust out, they were contentious and ungrateful. As previously stable agricultural communities became commercialized, and those too old or too unlucky to gain from the changes lost their place in the new communities, the cycle of ingratitude and accusation accelerated. The old, once respected for their cunning and experience, now became suspect. Increasingly, powerless women were progressively marginalized and simultaneously labeled as suspicious characters.

Another group of potential suspects were the providers of charms and folk remedies. When such remedies went bad, the customers who paid for the cures or the potions might conclude that the purveyor was at fault. In effect, suspicions of premodern folk medical malpractice became accusations of witchcraft. There is some evidence that the exercise of countermagic in England and New England was increasing in the seventeenth century, and learned authorities recognized the phenomenon. With it came an increasing number of rumors of witchcraft.

Such folk beliefs were subject to manipulation by the malign or the mischievous. So George Burroughs of Salem and Casco Bay, Maine, touted his own almost supernatural strength and his ability to hear conversations when he was not present. Neighbors noticed and credited him with special powers. Caleb Powell of Newbury, on the coast of Massachusetts, told his neighbors that he could find a witch "by his learning," thereby advertising his services. The exploitation of folk beliefs might be more malicious: the credulous might be tormented by a neighbor or a relative who was clever enough to conceal himself and his knavery. The victim would be assaulted by day with stones thrown by an assailant in hiding, and by night with strange noises, lights, and the rattle of pebbles on a roof. The victim might conclude that he or she was bewitched and, fearing that, become ill or distraught.

The most famous of these inversions of folk credulity was the haunting of William and Elizabeth Morse, of Newbury. Grandparents who had grown up in the town and were honored for their virtues, they undertook to rear a grandson, John Stiles. Stiles was evidently a difficult child who may have waged a campaign against his grandparents by tossing pots and pans about the house when they were not looking. Caleb Powell recognized what the child was doing and offered to intercede, perhaps to drum up business for himself as a cunning man. Once the lad was taken out of the house, its haunting ended. Unsatisfied, William Morse decided that Powell himself must have magical powers, and he accused Powell of bewitching the child. Meanwhile the neighbors, themselves frightened by the entire episode, began to voice suspicions about Elizabeth, claiming that she had a long history of causing harm, or at least of being close by when harm occurred. The result was a series of trials and the conviction and for a time the incarceration of Elizabeth, despite William's passionate defense of her innocence.

Powell saw the boy playing tricks and considered the cure simple: take the boy aside and make him stop. When Mary Warren, a servant in Salem, began to see specters of witches, her master, John Proctor, assayed the same solution as Powell's. As he told Samuel Sibley, a neighbor, at the height of the Salem crisis, Proctor "would his fetch his jade home and thrash the devil out of her." It worked until Warren went off to be with her friends, Mary Walcott, Mercy Lewis, and Elizabeth Hubbard. Children rebelling against a strict religious regimen might concoct among themselves a plot to misbehave and get away with it—if some supernatural agent could be blamed for their misfortunes. Thus the Reverend Joshua Moody, of the First Church of Boston, reported to Increase Mather the strange behavior of four children of Boston mason John Goodwin. They would cry out of sudden pains passing through various portions of their bodies and carry on in chorus. But "when the pain is over they eat, drink, walk, play, laugh as at other times [and] they are generally well at night." Moody continued that "physic" did not seem to help. Moody told Mather because he knew that Mather was collecting information on unusual occurrences to continue his essay on illustrious providences. Little did Moody realize that Increase's son Cotton would intervene, examine the children, and conclude that witchcraft was afoot. As a "critical eye-witness" he took Martha Goodwin into his own home and later interviewed in jail the convicted witch, an old Irish washerwoman named Mary Glover. Cotton Mather had none of his father's or Moody's hesitation—the younger Mather was a believer.

Fear of witches and the desire to punish witchcraft was not merely a private matter. Harmful magic was made a felony by statute in Tudor England in 1542. A more comprehensive act in 1563 required that "maleficium"—actual harm—accompany the act of using magic. In the statute of 1563, using witchcraft to search for lost treasure or to hurt or try to hurt people or destroy property was made punishable by one year in prison. Dispensing love potions earned a similar sentence. Conjuring evil spirits or causing the death of another became a capital offense. Scotland's King James VI, personally convinced that witchcraft had been used against him and his wife, wanted stiffer penalties, and a year after he ascended the throne of England as James I in 1603, Parliament obliged. Treasure hunting with witchery and casting spells intending to cause harm would earn life sentences, and all other witchcraft was punishable by hanging. Although the statutes stressed the criminality of making or seeking to make a pact with the Devil, threats and quarrels followed by actual harm were alleged in all cases that were passed on as "true bills" by grand juries. John Gaule, who wrote a popular account of witchcraft in 1646, argued strenuously that the authorities should not seek the death penalty unless both the pact with the Devil and real damage could be established, for he had just witnessed the hanging of many falsely accused witches in Essex.

Ministers like Parris, Cotton Mather, and Increase Mather might inveigh at lecture time against folk beliefs and propose that they, not unlettered cunning folk, be the authorities on witchcraft, but in fact they were often as credulous as their parishioners. The stories of ghosts that made the rounds of porches and parlors—the oral culture—resembled uncannily the stories of ghosts that the Mathers published in their popular books of remarkable occurrences. The ministerial elite had a special reason for following the track of the Devil and his minions, however. The leaders of the fellowship of ministers like Increase and Cotton Mather credited such tales because they were regarded as signs of God's plan. Even more important to the preachers, the witch who made a pact with the Devil (or thought she made such a pact, or even wanted to make such a pact) undermined the authority of the learned ministry. Thus John Davenport of New Haven warned against witches from his pulpit long before Cotton Mather was to make these warnings the centerpiece of his preaching, and minister George Moxon of Springfield accused witches of attacking his children nearly a half century before Samuel Parris came to the same conclusion. Suspected witchcraft was associated with irreligion, and irreligion could not be tolerated.

The written law in Massachusetts used the language of the Bible rather than the requirements of the English statutes to define the crime of witchcraft. The Body of Liberties of 1641, followed by the *Book of the Lawes and Liberties* of 1648, simply stated, "If any man or woman be a witch (that is hath or consulted with a familiar spirit) they shall be put to death." Witchcraft was contact with the Evil One rather than criminal acts against other people. Nevertheless, Massachusetts judges did not allow popular credulity or unsubstantiated rumor and innuendo to dictate the outcome of cases—not, at least, until the Salem trials. Cases were relatively few in number and isolated in space. Those that did occur were rooted in long-term suspicions against the accused. More often than not, the victims and the suspects were women. Each suspicion represented a long course of angry words and frustration, but none led to a witch-hunt like the European mass persecutions of the sixteenth century or the English prosecutions of the 1640s. Magistrates demanded proof, not presumption. Accused witches were more often than not acquitted, but they were also warned; for where there was suspicion, there was disorder, and Puritans did not want disorder. The accused witch had caused grief and should mend her ways.

Thus even though the fear of witches was shared by ordinary people and their betters, the magistrates had reined in popular passions—until the Salem outbreak. On this occasion, however, the suspicion of witchcraft fit into events occurring outside of Salem. The fear of witches rode the winds of war. A conflict between England and France beginning in Europe soon spread to the New England frontier and brought stark, unrelieved terror. Salem lay at the southern end of a region of marsh and wood open to raids by France's Indian allies. Like a picket line on a battlefield there stretched a line of towns against which moved the enemies of the British settlers—the eastern Abenaki, the Huron, and their dreaded French allies.

In these towns the fear of Indians was pervasive. News of renewed hostilities awakened a lightly slumbering memory of the carnage of the Wampanoag chief Metacom's uprising, called King Philip's War, barely a generation before. Although that war had ended in victory for the Puritans, nightmares from it remained. Everyone knew someone who had not come back from the yearlong war, but in 1692 Indians still strolled Salem's lanes, drank at back doors, and hunted in the nearby woods. Even more Indians lurked in the dark corners of Salem's imagination.

For the menfolk, the prospect of war on the frontier raised levels of anxiety and preparedness. They marshaled themselves, trained, and prepared to march off to defend the settlements. Women experienced war differently; they did not go off to war but were its victims nonetheless. They remembered what had happened in 1675 and 1676. Women and children on both sides had died in their homes or on familiar paths. No place had been safe.

Thus, the Salem Village region was gripped with panic and overrun with dreadful rumors in the winter of 1692. Salem was a way station on the road south from the settlements in New Hampshire and Maine. A steady stream of refugees fleeing Indian raids brought reports of massacres, firsthand accounts of fighting, and predictions of future savagery. There was enough truth to the stories to make the refugees celebrities of sorts, but they carried with them a kind of germ, the symptoms of which were frightening. They had seen terrors, and they terrified those who listened to them.

Merging the bits and pieces of stories from the north with their own imagined tales, the young people began to formulate a larger mythic structure—a fantasy world for themselves. Parents overheard and misunderstood. In trying to make sense for themselves of the childrens' stories, the parents reconfigured the elements of the story, making it a more conventional tale of witches and their victims. Palpable fear itself made Salem people readier to accept supernatural explanations for illness and misfortune.

It was this tension more than any other that made rumors of witchcraft so real. They flowed into other social pressures, of course. For example, in Andover, on Salem's northwestern border, a population boom put terrific pressure on what had been a well-functioning system of town land distribution. Too many sons and daughters overburdened that system, straining the social and emotional relationship that owning land reflected and reinforced. Andover was a patriarchy, with sons living well into their twenties on family farms. Fathers thus controlled their children, and children accepted that control, for good behavior would bring a patrimony and the chance to start one's own family on one's own farm. Large numbers of children living into adulthood threatened all that. It was not by accident that so many of the witches accused in the Salem crisis would come from Andover. But the first witches were espied in Salem Village.

CHAPTER 4

The Accusers

Had Betty's illness gone away, or had she been a poor farmer's daughter, the episode might have passed without event. But she was the minister's child. Her travail became the Village's preoccupation. Her parents and Tituba rallied to her, but her symptoms did not abate. Worse, her ailment seemed to have been contagious. Other girls in the neighborhood soon flew about, contorting themselves in pain, falling down in rigid postures, complaining of pinching and biting sensations. Visiting ministers said their piece, to no avail. Neighbors tried "white magic," but nothing came of it. The doctor was powerless. In the meantime Betty gained other comforters.

Tituba consoled Betty, later testifying that she loved her young charge, but Tituba's tales and customs were different from English folkways, and in times of trouble differences lead to suspicion and accusation. Black slaves in Puritan households had to live in a twilight world, neither theirs nor their masters'. In times of stress, slaves were obvious scapegoats for the unexplained and the inexplicable. Other slaves in Salem, Mary Black and Candy, for example, would become targets of witchcraft accusations later in the crisis. For now, Tituba had become the center of attention. Ironically and ultimately sadly for her, by participating in the episode of the witch cake, Tituba became more dangerous in the eyes of the Villagers. Some of them began to view her as a witch.

Betty's father cared for her, but they were not exactly friends. His attention was otherwise engaged, and he was not particularly sensitive in any case. In subtle ways Betty may have found her way to his side by playing the little mother and helpmate, but Samuel Parris was a demanding parent. Such fathers doled out love as a reward for obedience, dictated appropriate conduct to their children, and warned of parental and divine displeasure for those who disobeyed. Samuel Parris prayed with his girls, taught them to read and write, worried about their prospects, and in turn received deference from them. He anticipated that Betty would become a wife and mother, for which custom decreed the virtues of modesty, compliance, and deference—in all, inoffensive invisibility. As far as Samuel Parris was concerned, Betty's life was laid out for her.

Betty's mother offered love and comfort, but she was not a strong woman and had a toddler to care for. In fact, both Elizabeth Sr. and young Susannah would die before five years had passed. In her effort to succor Betty in her illness, Elizabeth Parris Sr. was not alone. Although a newcomer to the Village, she was soon surrounded by a literal and figurative circle of other women who visited, comforted, helped, and shared information. The ordinary boundaries of the woman's world rarely extended beyond home and garden, but visiting was an exception. Pathways through meadows to friends' houses and the cart track to the village center were always filled. Some of these visitors were older women, who offered the wisdom of their years to beleaguered mothers of sick children. Among the latter visitors were also cunning women, folk healers, who might prescribe herbal medicines or even suggest that the cause of a child's illness was not natural.

Betty's visitors included children from the neighboring homes. These girls, like her, were beginning to learn what was expected of them later in life. If they were Betty's age or younger, they still faced the long passage from the openness of childhood to the subtleties of adulthood. At nine or ten, girls gained their own identity in the records of court and town—a name of their own and responsibilities as well. Nevertheless, the gap between childhood and adulthood yawned perilously deep. For some girls the passage would be fraught with betrayal and uncertainty, causing them emotional and physical pain.

Betty's friends provided the critical context for Betty's illness and the accusations of witchcraft that were to follow. Betty played with her cousin Abigail, who shared the house, and the girls practiced some fortune-telling. They looked into a cup filled with milk and egg to find out who they might marry (the most important subject in their lives), and there, the story goes, saw a coffin, which terrified them. Soon after, both girls fell ill. The coffin symbolized death, but Betty and Abigail had seen coffins already. Death was very near all these girls. Epidemic diseases like smallpox and typhoid regularly carried off the young. So did the French and Indian raids. The Puritans had learned to prepare their children for death; indeed, they harped on the nearness of it.

To the girls, it was not the coffin itself but the fear that they had violated Samuel Parris's rules that made them ill. They had played with the Devil's tools, and Parris had told them that the Devil was always waiting to trap the unwary and the unregenerate. The pinches they felt thereafter were self-inflicted punishments, anticipating both the appearance of a demon hungry for their souls and an adult angry at their transgressions. (Pinching was a common form of corporal punishment Puritans administered to their erring young.)

Betty and Abigail played with other girls in the neighborhood, and these playmates must have become curious about the two little girls' sudden illness. Down the road a mile lived Thomas and Ann Putnam, with bright little Ann Jr., twelve, and Mercy Lewis, their seventeen-year-old servant. Nearer still were Elizabeth Hubbard, the niece of Dr. Griggs, who was also his maid; Mary Walcott, the daughter of Parris's neighbor and Putnam brother-in-law Jonathan; and John Proctor's servant Mary Warren. The illness soon fashioned a crude ring around the girls in unintended parody of the domestic circle of their mothers and aunts.

The number of afflicted would grow, but these seven remained the core. They knew each other, and although their relations were framed in part by their social status, the social hierarchy was flat at the top. Betty and Ann Putnam occupied the highest rank, but they were the youngest of the group, and, even more important, neither a minister's child nor a well-to-do farmer's daughter could afford to sneer at other children. Mary Walcott was a common farmer's daughter, but her family worked its own land. Williams, Hubbard, and Lewis were household servants, but domestic service was often part of the life course— the natural cycle of life—of a Puritan girl, and they might make a good marriage later in life. The friendships were fairly new (Betty and Abigail had moved into the neighborhood only a few years before) and therefore somewhat fragile, but the youngsters had a good deal in common.

The girls' circle was bounded by conversations and confidences. Stories were no doubt embroidered and expanded as the girls used anecdotes and yarns to bond to one another. Such friendships involve fantasy, secret sharing, and periodic tests of loyalty. The girls felt uneasy when speaking to parents and ministers, but among themselves they could speak freely, letting their imaginations and their storytelling skills range freely. Tales of witchery and omens, danger and heroism brought down from the forests and the frontier titillated the girls that winter of 1692; the group performances these girls later put on during the examinations of suspected witches merely expanded upon the verbal games they had perfected weeks and months before.

Yet, even after they accused their neighbors by name of the terrible crime of witchcraft, the girls might not have realized the severity of their conduct. Angry neighbors often accused each other of being "Satan's toads" or wished that someone would "go to the Devil," and nothing official happened to the accuser or the accused. There had been no trials for witchcraft in the girls' neighborhood in their lifetimes. In Boston, four years before, Mary Glover had gone to the gallows for bewitching the children of John Goodwin, and adults in Salem knew the story well. But Salem was far from Boston, and the girls probably did not realize how well they mimicked Goodwin's young ones. The girls understood that witchcraft was a horrid crime whose punishment was death, but so was false accusation a dreadful crime, as their ministers and parents reminded them. It too was punishable by death under the old charter, but this dire fate did not deter them. They spun out fantasy, and fantasy so enveloped them that its consequences were lost in the fog.

Nor did their minister press them to recant. The church and its minister were supposed to be the first line of defense against false witness. When a parishioner was suspected of lying, ministers were expected to inquire, counsel, and arrange for public apology. Public lying in a face-to-face society had a devastating effect on those it injured and on those who told the lie. John Hale, Parris's counterpart in Beverly, recalled one case that should have taught everyone a lesson (though he recalled it five years too late to change the course of the witchcraft trials): when a Watertown, Massachusetts, nurse told a lie that resulted in another woman being accused of witchcraft, God punished the liar. Jailed for her own adultery, the nurse had her baseborn child, then died. In Beverly, Hale himself cross-examined one of the witnesses against George Burroughs when he was accused of witchcraft in May 1692, demanding that the witness recant if anything she said was untrue, for bearing false witness was an unpardonable sin. The witness avowed that she had indeed seen Burroughs presiding over a Devil's Sabbath in the Village. Parris had an affirmative duty to warn the girls that they must not lie. Still, they persisted, and he did not curb them. Indeed, he supported them once they had gone public.

For the girls, what had begun in playful terror, the same sort of simulated horror that modern teenagers experience—indeed, seek to experience—at amusement parks and in movie theaters, became something else entirely. Nineteenth-century historians thought the girls were shamming or using tricks. The girls' parents could have reached the same conclusion, if they had wanted to repudiate the stories of their own children. Seventeenth-century English books and pamphlets documented occasions when children, to excuse themselves from past mischief, claimed that witches were the cause. Puritan literature warned of the usual signs of such feigning in children: lying, profanity, truancy, and playing games.

There is a more disturbing possibility about the causes of the girls' distress that cannot be proved but ought not be dismissed out of hand. The abuse of children by adults in their household is too well documented now to be ignored, particularly when the victims begin to act out aggressive fantasies or show other common symptoms like excessive blaming and humiliation, frightening accusations, and name-calling. This is the very conduct that the girls adopted that winter long ago in Salem. Historians have found that abuse of children and servants was common, if not epidemic, in the Massachusetts colony. The girls' first reports in these cases at times resemble the testimony in modern child abuse cases.

What makes truth and fantasy in all such abuse cases difficult to assess for people in the community is that the same investigatory process that reveals the hidden crime may induce false accusations. In modern child abuse cases, anxious parents (or if the parents themselves are accused, school, church, and civil authorities) may so prompt and otherwise give cues to the putative victims that the accusations become a product of the inquisitor's coaching. Single incidents of no real import may be altered in the child's mind, either through confusion or through the desire to please questioners, into detailed accounts of abuse. The stronger the interrogator's belief, the more he or she will demand confirmation from the child, and the more likely the child, especially a suggestible one, will be to provide that testimony.

Were words put in the Salem girls' mouths? That is the problem of evidence in modern child abuse cases, and it is very similar to the problem the parents and ministers faced in Salem. There is evidence that parents, ministers, and later government officials helped the girls to fashion their story, in effect molding it into accepted categories of witchcraft. There is no evidence of sexual abuse, but it was not uncommon, particularly among young women in situations such as those of Hubbard, Lewis, and Warren. In the end, the possibility of child abuse remains a tantalizing hypothesis and nothing more.

Whether the girls began as mischievous innocents manipulated by parents and other adults or as victims of overbearing Puritan discipline, they soon had turned themselves from a circle of friends into what modern observers might recognize as a gang of juvenile delinquents. Such groups were not unknown in Puritan Massachusetts, but only bits and pieces of their ganglike conduct come to light in the court records. Gangs attract young people who are disaffected from the mores of their elders, and in the 1680s ministers and magistrates moaned that their children lacked the piety and purpose that marked the founders' generation. Everywhere these ministers found young ones mocking the values and virtues of their parents, wearing their hair too long, walking unescorted at night, dancing in public places, and mingling indiscriminately with members of the opposite sex. The Puritans had discovered juvenile delinquency in their midst, and they were appalled.

Perhaps the group of girls in the Village had no leader, or rather, leadership shifted from one to another of the girls. Such loose packs of adolescents and near adolescents are more common than structured gangs. The line separating the diffuse pack from the general population is almost invisible in real life. Those in the pack share romance, fantasy, and excitement—indeed, they may pose for each other tests just like those the girls created when they took turns describing the witches' spectral flights during the hearings to come.

Once constituted, the group developed its own ranking system. Packs and gangs have hierarchies that are internal as well as external, and often the two do not match. Nine-year-old Betty and eleven-year-old Abigail and Ann could not lead the older girls. Mary Warren was old enough to lead, but she was an unwilling participant in the activities of the accusers, and later she attempted to recant her testimony. In the process, she demonstrated that she feared the other girls, an unlikely admission for a leader. Hubbard, Walcott, and Susannah Sheldon, an occasional member of the pack, were in their late teens, but they were not the leaders, for if one examines their testimony in the pretrial hearings, one finds it imitative and uninventive. They followed what others said. What is more, Sheldon and Hubbard were not always part of the indictments, unlike Putnam, Williams, and one other girl—Mercy Lewis.

Lewis was old enough to influence the others; indeed, she may have brought Putnam into the circle. A servant, she had to be out and about more than the younger girls. More important, unlike the other girls, she did not need to fantasize about terror. She had seen her parents die in an Indian raid. Such experiences alienate a child, leaving a sense of anger and betrayal in their wake. Finally, there was her testimony. Of all the girls, she was far and away the most forceful, imaginative, and compelling in her accusations. But Lewis did not always lead; the girls passed that task around.

To continue in existence, an important motive for all pack and gang members, the girls had to find ways to conform their activities to the values of the community. No gang or pack can survive without at least passive acquiescence from those in authority. The girls' witchcraft accusations gave many in Salem a chance to affirm that something was wrong with their lives and that someone or something was to blame. In more complex ways, the entire process of seeking out witches enabled the community to restate its moral expectations. The ferreting out of suspected deviants not only kept the Devil at bay but also brought people together in rituals of self-purgation, at least so long as villagers believed what the girls said. Thus what the girls did was useful and even encouraged. Not just to gain attention for themselves but to keep their group in being, they continued to name new witches and acted out the afflictions of the bewitched.

When they denounced people as witches, they were generally careful to name men and women who were not near neighbors. They did not find witches in the Village center, among those who lived closest to the parsonage. Instead, at first, they saw the specters of Sarah Good, whose home was wherever someone would house her, her laborer husband, her infant, and her four-year-old daughter. The girls also named Sarah Osborn, whose house was almost two miles away, north of Wolf Pits Meadow; Sarah Cloyse, who resided to the northeast of Osborn, on Frost Fish Creek; John and Elizabeth Proctor, who dwelled two miles south of the training fields, at the foot of Felton's Hill; Giles and Martha Corey, whose home was two miles to the southwest, at the end of Proctor's Brook; and Bridget Bishop, whose ill fame had spread from Salem town when she married Edward Bishop in 1685 and moved to a house two and a half miles up the Ipswich Road from the Village. She testified at her hearing that she had never been to the Village's center, a fact no one contested. The only two supposed witches the girls denounced who lived in the girls' immediate vicinity were Tituba, who as a slave had no legal standing in the community, and Rebecca Nurse, whose family was engaged in a long-standing quarrel with the Putnams.

When they had canvassed the likely suspects in Salem, they had to disband the group or seek out new fields to conquer. In April they looked to Topsfield, where they found Abigail and Deliverance Hobbs, Sarah Wildes, and Elizabeth Howe, the last, like Cloyse, Nurse, and their sister Mary Esty (all born into the Townes family), kin to families with whom the Putnams had quarreled. In May they found Andover's Martha Carrier, who, they must have heard, few in Andover liked. A month later the request of Andover's Joseph Ballard, son of one of the town founders, brought Ann Jr. and Mary Walcott to Andover, where, blindfolded, they were touched by a parade of men and women suspected of bewitching Ballard's dying wife. Four they named as witches, all the while relishing the role of wandering witchfinders. When the girls were finished in Andover, its citizens started accusing each other—resulting in a grand total of forty-one accused from the town.

The girls had become good listeners, and the adults around them inadvertently provided cues to the identity of men and women suspected of deviant ways or unpopular beliefs. Among these latter were the Quakers of Essex County, long persecuted and in 1692 only barely tolerated. The girls found these men and women ready targets, for was not "quaking" akin to possession by a demon? In 1660, when Quakers faced death for persisting in their heresy, Massachusetts judges had told the defendants that their crime was, "like witchcraft," a rebellion against God and the colony. As it happened, among the Salem accused, Elizabeth Proctor's family had Quaker connections, and Francis and Rebecca Nurse had adopted a Quaker son. A number of the Andover suspects also had Quaker affiliations.

When the ranks of the commoners were depleted, the girls turned their attention to the elite of Salem and the colony. When the trials were under way, the crown prosecutor Thomas Newton was impressed with how high their accusations reached, for "the afflicted spare no person of what quality soever, neither conceale their crimes tho never so hainous." They began with their masters, Mary Warren naming John and Elizabeth Proctor, and Sarah Churchill, another of the girls' followers, offering an indictment of her master, George Jacobs Sr. By May the girls were accusing Philip and Mary English, a rich immigrant merchant (he had changed his name from L'Anglois) and his wife, and John Alden, a Boston sea captain turned trader. Both men were quite comfortable in court—English was a veteran litigator, to judge from the court records, and Alden feared no one, not even the governor—but both fled until the crisis was over. Later rumor had the girls accusing the wife of the governor, but that rumor circulated when the crisis had passed.

CHAPTER 5

The Magistrates and the Suspects

Sometime between February 25, when Tituba fed the witch cake to an unsuspecting dog, and February 29, when an arrest warrant was issued, Betty and Abigail named their afflictors: Tituba, Sarah Good, and Sarah Osborn. Betty told her parents that the girls had been approached by the Devil; when they rejected His offer, His witches began their assault. Abigail confirmed the story.

With Betty's words the witch-hunt began, but in the end she proved the least aggressive of the girls. Adults translated for her and prodded her, seeking more evidence of a conspiracy of witches, but then her parents delayed, once again advised to be patient by intercessors like the Reverend John Hale of Beverly. Parris hesitated because he believed that children were born in original sin and their nature was evil. Instruction, loving care, and wise counsel could lead them toward the light, but perhaps, even after all he had seen and despite his belief in the power of witches, the girls were lying. One final motive stayed his hand: he was still the outsider, and he knew it. Let others take the lead in such matters.

Although the adults had allowed, indeed encouraged, the girls to name the witches, there was still time for reconciliation. Parents and ministers might have refused to believe the girls or urged them not to cast aspersions. But the Putnams would not wait. Frustrated by their falling status in the town and their economic failures, they saw in the whispers of witchcraft a possible source of their decline. Ann Putnam Jr.'s father, Sergeant Thomas, his brother-in-law Joseph Hutchinson, and brother Edward Putnam went to Salem to file an information with the magistrates against Good, Osborn, and Tituba. Of course, the magistrates could have pooh-poohed the accusations, but the Putnams were not a clan to be trifled with. The die was cast.

As Betty's parents gently but firmly pushed her off center stage, little Ann Putnam, urged on by her father and mother, assumed a starring role. Over time, different girls would take the lead, but the local eminence of Ann's family gave urgency to the proceedings. When the interrogations began, it was the Putnam clan that sat by their girls, took notes, encouraged the clerk and the justices of the peace, and put their weight behind the prosecutions. The Putnam elders signed depositions stating that they had witnessed the girls' suffering. The other adolescent accusers were related to the Putnams: Ann Jr., a daughter, and Ann Sr., the wife of Thomas; Mary Walcott, a niece; Mercy Lewis, a servant in their home; Elizabeth Hubbard, the servant and grandniece of supporter and client William Griggs; and Mary Walcott, the daughter of brother-in-law Jonathan Walcott. Over time, more girls came forward, like Susannah Sheldon and Sarah Churchill, who lived and worked in the Village but were not part of the Putnam clan, and some adults, like the notoriously bad-tempered midwife Sarah Bibber. Later, some of the accused confessed, but the support of the senior Putnams was vital to the first round of accusations and remained so throughout the crisis.

Betty's and Abigail's accusations were so similar in form and substance that either the three women did visit the girls in spectral form or the girls worked out their tales together. The uniformity of the details in the girls' stories is a common sign of plagiarism. Very shortly thereafter, little Ann Putnam Jr. and Mercy Lewis saw the same three witches flying through the winter mist. The girls in the two households must have talked among themselves. We have seen how the ordinary social intercourse of girls could transform itself into such fabrications.

These first accusations were hesitant, as if the girls were afraid to name the witches. If there really were witches, such caution would make sense. The witch might take vengeance. But assuming the girls were telling lies, why did accusation come so hard for them? If we look at the women who later confessed to being witches (some of whom still later recanted the confessions), we get a new insight into the minds of the girls. The key is that the audience for the confessions and accusations was not the world of the girls or their mothers but important adult men. The girls wanted to control their world, and at the same time they wanted to please the adult male authority figures by telling those men what they evidently sought to hear. The delay gave the girls a chance not only to rehearse the details of their story but also to figure out what their audience wanted in that story—precisely the same thought process that motivated the adult confessors.

What is more, the girls were capable of feeling guilty. They knew that they were lying, even if they could not predict the mortal consequences of the lies in the days to come. At various times, particularly early in the crisis, these girls must have shared something of the sense of sinfulness that apparently motivated the women who confessed to being witches even though they were no such thing. Late-seventeenth-century Massachusetts was a tightly wound, highly moralistic place. Everyone felt guilty about something in their lives—an inner conviction that he or she had failed to come up to the mark. Ordinary sins of greed, covetousness, wantonness, and anger must have preceded extraordinary sins like making a pact with the Devil, or He would not have spent so much time in Salem and its environs. The young accusers hesitated because they feared the Devil as much as anyone.

Given that the girls had little option in their own minds but to name someone, Tituba was an obvious and perhaps even inevitable choice. She had already become the focus of suspicion. No doubt they had heard Parris blame Tituba, for later Tituba was reported to have accused Parris of beating her to get a confession. Once named, Tituba had little defense. A slave, she was visibly, socially, and legally an outsider. Who could speak for her? Her master might, but he was already looking in her direction with suspicion in his eyes.

But why name anyone else? Here we might speculate that each of the girls wanted to contribute something to the common tale. Abigail may have decided on Tituba (perhaps jealous that Betty was always Tituba's favorite). Other girls selected Good and Osborn. Good was a disreputable beggar. Osborn was old; Joseph Putnam sympathetically called her "gamar" in his notes, a common form of address for older women, and one connoting the close if ambivalent tie between nurturing and witchcraft in New England. Both women were suspected of practicing witchcraft for a long time before 1692, and both had lost husbands to suspicious causes.

When the Putnams brought their suspicions to county magistrates Jonathan Corwin and John Hathorne, the justices of the peace issued warrants for the women named by the girls and arranged for an inquest. Hathorne and Corwin were not Village men, but they knew the Village and its denizens. Both men were merchants, Corwin the son of one of Salem's first great merchants; Hathorne, whose family was equally venerable in the story of the town, the son of a successful farmer. They were also veteran politicians whose duties included serving as justice of the peace and county judge. Both were familiar with the Village's troubles. Both had opposed severing the Village from the town, pitting them against the Putnams. Hathorne was related by marriage to the Porters, but the relation had deprived him of land (his father, William Hathorne, had given it to the girls as dowry). More important for later events, both magistrates believed that the Devil could use witches to undermine the church and to hurt people, sharing ordinary folk notions of the invisible world.

The surviving legal record of these examinations can be read as a dramatic script. Folk wisdom, book law, and a lifetime of living with one another among a people used to talking and listening wrote that script. The magistrates added to it two sober but credulous characters. In effect, everyone said their lines. Although differences in social and economic status were important for the speakers, their common fear of witches was of greater consequence. Even the men and women wrongly accused of witchcraft believed in the power of witches to harm the innocent.

And everyone had their part. For the magistrates, the hearings were tests of their authority and judgment. They must ferret out a deadly conspiracy before it struck at them or their children. For the suspects, even more was at stake in this performance. Some, particularly those against whom no prior accusation had been lodged, expressed bewilderment. They tried to talk the girls out of their accusations and the magistrates out of their suspicions. Others, accustomed to being suspected of something by their neighbors, acted hostile and cynical. They professed their innocence with a hard-edged disregard for the whole proceeding. Some of the witnesses' parts were the most difficult and moving, for testifying forced them to recall moments when they had come face-to-face with an apparition or a strange and horrifying animal. The memory was painful, and its recital at the examination of the suspects might arouse the dormant enmity of a witch. The Putnam clan hovered nearby. Although they did not speak much, they watched and listened. Everyone at the hearings had to run a gauntlet of Putnams.

Other witnesses were friends, loved ones, and families of the suspects. They gave aid by their mere presence, and on occasion they offered character testimonials.

The examination of the suspects began on March 1, in Ingersoll's tavern, but so many came to see the show that it was moved to the meetinghouse down the road. Corwin and Hathorne sat on one side of the communion table, with their backs to the wall of the meetinghouse. Witnesses and accused milled about on the other side. The communion table had great significance in its meetinghouse setting, for the Lord's Supper was the most important sacrament and defined Puritan piety. Testifying before the Lord's table, the girls had a credibility they might not have had if they stood next to the dirty, knife-gouged tables of Ingersoll's tavern.

In the meetinghouse the two magistrates watched the girls' performance for the first time. The girls seemed to be bitten and pinched by invisible agents. In visible and audible agony, the victims twisted their arms and backs and contorted their faces. Sometimes they could not speak; other times they could not stop speaking. Most of those who watched were filled with compassion and became fully convinced that the girls were truly afflicted. In one sense, the girls' fits and spasms were familiar. Children, women, and men possessed or attacked by evil sprites often had fits. Leading New England ministers like Increase and Cotton Mather wrote books and gave sermons about these episodes, and, as John Hale noted, the accounts were widely read.

But were the girls afflicted by witches? And were those witches the ones they named? In front of the magistrates, the girls' afflictions initiated a legal proceeding from which there was no turning back. On March 1, mere suffering whose origin may or may not have been devilish changed into formal evidence of a serious crime. The conventionality of the girls' fits had allowed parents and other caretakers to reconfigure otherwise frightening events as familiar ones, and so cope with them, but no one need face the noose for doing the girls harm until the magistrates arrived. Once the magistrates started taking testimony, the girls' tormented accusations turned illness—and playacting—into proof of wrongdoing.

The magistrates heard the accusations under their commissions as justices of the peace. Their authority was written, based on textual models taken from English books of forms, but the informality of the hearings, the close physical proximity and intimate social relationships among all the participants, and the vividness of the girls' testimony gave substance to the accusations more than did any books of forms. Imagine a theater-in-the-round wherein everyone—actors, writers, director, audience—performs an arm's-length away from the audience and the audience takes part in the show. Good actors can convince a willing audience that the actor can see what the audience cannot see. The girls persuaded the townspeople and the authorities of the reality of invisible witches.

Of course, the effectiveness of the girls' performance depended upon the credulity of the audience. Men and women in Salem were ready to believe in the girls because they had long harbored suspicions of some of their neighbors, and by early April the girls were joined by a variety of adults who remembered strange episodes from past years, sometimes twenty or thirty years before. Before the magistrates these older men now came, for men predominated among the latter group as women predominated among the afflicted. The men recalled wooing that had failed, cheese and butter mysteriously gone bad, oddly shaped animals suddenly appearing and frightening people, and terrifying unnatural events. When these older men came to court, they were discharging a function the community expected them to discharge, for Salem Village, though literate, needed its elders to recall the past. They did not come out of malice, because the affliction was fresh in their minds, or because the damage was still unrepaired but because it was their job to recount the common history of the people. With their testimony, oral folk customs came to dominate the formal hearings of a legally constituted tribunal.

Such customs had served the people of Salem well in the past, but nothing in the experience of the men and women of the town prepared them for what was happening to them now. Before the Salem cases, neighbors tried to be careful about what they said about one another, and when one person maliciously or falsely accused another of some offense, magistrates ordered public confessions of error to bring communities together again. In the heat of argument, Essex men and women did tell each other to go to the Devil, as Martha Corey shouted at a neighbor during a dispute over milk cows. Between 1672 and 1692, the Essex County courts heard forty cases involving slanderous charges and countercharges of devilment. How many more there must have been that did not end in litigation is anyone's guess.

When neighbors did not mean to cast aspersions, they took pains to say so. During the inquiry into the cases of Hugh and Mary Parsons, Jonathan Taylor deposed that he called Goody Merick "a witch" because she was able to open a beer keg tap that he, with all his might, could not budge, but he hastened to add, "but I would not have you think it was by witchery." Taylor was well aware that the usage of ordinary people could be taken quite differently when given in evidence in a criminal trial.

Women publicly accused of witchcraft might respond with a countersuit for defamation or slander. Uncorrected by him, Taylor's words might have led to such a suit. Mary Parsons had been sued by the widow Marshfield for saying that after the widow came to Springfield, there were unexplained lights in the meadow at night, and worse, that perhaps the widow had "witched away" the wool that Parsons was supposed to bring to a neighbor's house. Husbands filed such suits on behalf of their wives. For example, in 1650 Erasmus James brought suit for his wife against Peter Pitford. Pitford had gone about telling his friends that Goodwife James had sailed off to Boston in a boat and, once safely at sea, turned herself into a cat. His listeners believed him, at least to the extent of passing the rumor on to others. James won fifty shillings from Peter upon a jury verdict. In similar cases for which verdicts survive, Massachusetts plaintiffs won fourteen; defendants prevailed but three times. Defamers had to pay a fine and confess error.

The courts also found ways to deflect accusations. They simply treated the supposed necromancer or witch as a liar and fined him or her accordingly. In September 1652 John Broadstreet of Rowley was presented by a grand jury for having familiarity with the Devil, but the justices fined him instead for lying repeatedly about his prowess. Broadstreet's explanation to the court was clever—he had tried to trick the Devil, not obey Him. He was reading a book of magic when he heard a voice ask him what work he did. Fearing that he was being addressed by the Devil, he answered smartly: go make a bridge of sand over the ocean, then a ladder of sand up to heaven, and finally, ascend the ladder, "goe to God," and come back no more. Thus the Devil would stand before His judge, and Massachusetts would be safe. The court was not amused.

None of these timeworn methods to deflect slander worked in Salem in 1692, for Salem Village was so distraught over local turmoil and the colony was so disordered by war and political uncertainty that everyone believed the Devil was close at hand. Without these informal controls on superstition and bad feeling, the formal system of law had no way to sort fact from overheated fiction. The suspects confronted their accusers and could summon their own witnesses, but they could not disprove what the girls said. They could sneer at the girls or pity them, in effect accusing the girls of lying or being sick, or admit that the girls were bewitched but insist that they were mistaken about the identity of their assailants. Nevertheless, without formal legal advisers or patrons in the community, devoid of experience with the courts in matters of such moment, the first suspects must have found the examination frightening.

Good and Osborn stood firm—they were not witches. Good was bitter and mistrusted the magistrates. In counterpoint to her whining denials, the children, Betty, Abigail, Elizabeth Hubbard, and Ann Putnam Jr., screamed and writhed as if on cue. Hathorne, the primary questioner, knew Good's reputation and was harsh with her. She gave back venom. He belittled her, and she became confused. Historians have concluded that Hathorne believed that Good was guilty. No doubt he did, but his persistent style of interrogation, repeating the same question over and over, was not uncommon or surprising. It is a standard tactic of all good inquisitors, and Puritan prosecutors routinely used it. Convinced of the charges upon evidence, a magistrate was to press a suspect, examining "strictly." The suspect was not to be allowed to stand mute but must respond. In previous years both Hathorne and his father had gained reputations as intimidating interrogators, but their conduct here was no different from that of modern prosecuting attorneys. Hathorne assumed that Good knew enough to be more forthcoming than she had been, but his real purpose was to elicit a confession, without which, despite all the testimony of neighbors and the girls' contortions, no conviction was sure. Good's final, exhausted concession rewarded Hathorne's persistence. Asked who it was, if not she, who pinched the children, Good said, "[I]t was Sarah Osborn." The children concurred.

Osborn was older than her fifty calendar years and sick, housebound for much of the winter. Confronted with the girls' torment, she denied that she had harmed them. Perhaps the Devil had assumed her form. Asked by Hathorne if she knew Good, she said she did not, plainly meaning that Good was nothing more than a casual acquaintance. Hathorne, always looking for a conspiracy of witches, asked when Osborn had last seen Good—as if the two had flown together to the most recent witches' Sabbath. Osborn, obviously too ill to fly anywhere, replied that she had seen Good years before, in town. Well, then, Hathorne sprung at her, what did you call Good then? "Sarah," replied Osborn.

She was plainly tired but capable of some spunk. Were she not accused of witchcraft, Hathorne ought to have been properly abashed, for Puritanism valued the old and godly, but he had learned that she had not attended church for over a year. Why had she avoided going to meeting? The answer must have been written on her wretched face: she had been sick. A quarrelsome woman by all accounts, she was at the end of her tether. A mirror of the casual cruelty of these examinations: although she was not likely to flee the jurisdiction, the magistrates, upon the girls' testimony, ordered her imprisoned, where she died on May 10, denied the comfort of her own room and bed.

Osborn's case raised a new question that Hathorne was unwilling or unable to confront. Her first husband was Robert Prince, a Salem Village man, and her in-laws were Lieutenant Thomas Putnam and Captain John Putnam. When her first husband died, he made his Putnam kin the executors of his estate. Sarah Prince broke the connection to the Putnam clan when she married her indentured servant, Alexander Osborn, an Irish immigrant. When the elder son of the first marriage reached his majority, the Putnams sought to settle him in his inheritance, but the Osborns resisted, and the parties grew quarrelsome. She had been an outsider when she married Prince, and now she threatened to disinherit two Salem Village lads. Seen in this context, the accusation became a dispute over land waged by other means.

When at last Tituba was called, she denied any complicity. Had she remained adamant, Good and Osborn might well have been admonished and the affair ended. Hale thought that Tituba's confession "encouraged those in authority to examine others that were suspected."

But she could not predict the future. She recognized that she was in peril. Between the time that she baked the cake and the magistrates, summoned by the Putnams, arrived, Tituba had been questioned by Hale and other ministers and had admitted that "[h]er mistress in her own Country was witch, and had taught her some means to be used for the discovery of a witch and for the prevention of being bewitched, etc. But said that she herself was not a witch."

Historians have read Hale to mean that Tituba had learned some countermagic in Barbados, but what English plantation mistress would take aside a young slave and teach her magic, much more confess to the slave that a mistress could be a witch? One cannot just accept Hale's recounting; there was more to Tituba's story. She knew that suspicion was already falling on her and that she could become a scapegoat for the girls' suffering. Tituba had to protect herself—no one else would. Questioned in private by the ministers, she had a chance to try out an alibi—the story of the mistress's witchcraft. This was not pure fabrication. A confession must be believable; it must convince the inquisitor. If she admitted that she had learned how to bake the cake from her neighbors in Salem who knew and practiced plenty of countermagic, then she must inform on them, and this she was not ready to do, at least until it proved necessary. Instead, her "mistress in her own country" was the culprit.

Her first line of defense came crashing down when the magistrates arrived and simply refused to believe her. Seeing quite clearly that continued denials would not move them, Tituba admitted that she had been approached by a tall, strong man from Boston with white hair. He told her he was God, and she was afraid. Sometimes he wore dark coats. Other times he appeared as a dog or a hog. The magistrates assumed he was the Devil. Tituba confirmed that Good and Osborn were witches, described their "familiars" in terms the girls had already used, and added that she and four witches flew on poles through the air. She conceded that she had pinched the girls but did it only in fear of her own life.

It is certainly possible that she was so frightened by the proceedings that she allowed the magistrates to feed her the lines, but she seems to have managed better than a mere victim. Indeed, she had found a way to manipulate her accusers—the girls—and her masters. By confessing, Tituba had made herself a central figure in the inquiry. Next, she blended African with European witchcraft lore to give flesh to her fantasy. The mysterious man could turn into an animal, a power that African witches shared with English witches. The tall man was clearly white, though later accounts would make him tawny or black. The man approached her from out of nowhere. He had power. She could not dodge him. What was she to do?

Tituba's story proved that she had been coerced into cooperating with the man in black. Approached by him, she ran to Parris for advice, but the fearsome man blocked her path. Confused and afraid, she made her mark in the strange man's book, and he told her that it contained Osborn's and Good's names, along with seven others. At last, when the magistrates wanted more than she could fabricate, she claimed that her sight had failed. She had lost her powers, again controlling what they could do to her. Although she was examined the next day, the magistrates got no more from her. In saying that she had lost her sight, she defied the magistrates not only by refusing to answer further but also by calling upon West African custom to frame that refusal. There, a witch who was discovered and condemned lost her powers, including her special sight.

She had implicated others in the crime, which was exactly what the two justices of the peace both wanted and feared, for Hathorne and Corwin knew that witches usually acted in concert with other witches. Two years before, a runaway slave named Robert had testified that he was off to join a French and Indian expedition against the colony and he expected other Indians and blacks to join him. There was no expedition or general uprising, but because his story fed the authorities' worst nightmare, it was for a time credited. Tituba was not able to name the others (of course she had no inkling of who they might be, having just fabricated an entire coven of witches), and for the time being the magistrates were satisfied.

The suspects were jailed, but Salem was not quiet. How could it be, when there were still witches (four by Tituba's reckoning) flying around at night? On March 11 Ann Putnam was afflicted by the other witches. Three days later, Abigail Williams was attacked by the same spectral forms. Soon the accusers of Good, Osborn, and Tituba fastened upon Martha Corey and Rebecca Nurse, older women in the Village who, unlike their predecessors, were members in good standing of churches and apparently led upright lives. Both Corey and

Nurse, warned by their neighbors, regarded the girls' antics as the prattling of malice, but the men who went from house to house seeking evidence for the accusations, watching the faces and gestures of the new suspects, either did not see or would not credit the older women's view of the new accusations. Corey's sarcastic dismissal and Nurse's earnest bewilderment at the charges did not deter the growing number of unofficial witchfinders.

Parris and his fellow ministers still could have interceded, but their former caution was now replaced with zeal. When Deodat Lawson visited Salem Village and preached in the meetinghouse on the afternoon of March 20, Abigail Williams sat with the other girls. At the morning sermon Abigail had been contentious and spiteful, but in the afternoon she went further. She cried out, "Look where Goodwife Cloyse [Nurse's sister] sits on the Beam suckling her Yellow Bird between her fingers." Ann Putnam boldly added that the yellow bird had flown to Lawson's hat, but sensing that she had gone too far, those sitting nearby hushed her. Williams and Putnam basked in the attention of the bewildered congregation. The girls changed a place of worship into a theater of accusation; they had turned the auditory—the place where the congregation was to hear the minister—into a place where the Villagers had to listen to two girls.

After hearkening to the girls' wailing and watching them point fingers of accusation, Lawson preached an ambiguous sermon to the Salem congregation. The message was simple: pray, pray, pray, and it neatly fit both the jeremiad—the call to return to the older, purer faith of the founders of New England—and the way in which Puritans, from late in the sixteenth century, set out to combat the Devil's works. Lawson maintained that the Evil One had come to Salem. They were all in the Lion's jaws. To the Devil and those who had chosen to follow Him, the righteous must give no quarter. Christ had defeated the Devil, and so would the true in spirit.

What he said and what his audience made of it, however, were quite different. He was confident of final victory through prayer and good living, but some in the pews came away shaken. Ann Putnam Sr., little Ann's mother, was particularly disturbed, and she adopted Lawson's language to bring her own accusation before the magistrates. The elder Putnam was susceptible to suggestion. She had lost a six-week-old child, little Sarah, who would have been Ann Jr.'s younger sister, and evidently still grieved. A week before Lawson preached, Putnam, exhausted from her daughter's indisposition and her maid's complaints, lay down for a nap and was beset by the specter of witches. She recognized them as they pressed upon her chest. One was Martha Corey, the other Rebecca Nurse. The assault on Ann Sr. abated on the Sabbath but returned in full fury when the day of worship was done. This time, Nurse did more than pummel Putnam; Nurse insisted that Christ had no power to save the anguished mother. The threat had taken on theological dimensions. After hearing Lawson preach, Putnam swore to the magistrates that only God had delivered her "out of the jaws of those roaring lions"—the very words that Lawson had used in the meetinghouse.

The girls' targets were not just older women. On March 23 Samuel Brabrook, the town marshal's deputy, arrested four-year-old Dorcas Good on the order of Hathorne and Corwin. Lewis, Walcott, and Ann Putnam Jr. all testified that the specter of the child had bitten and pinched them. Little Dorcas was jailed in Salem, where on March 26, Hathorne, Corwin, and John Higginson arrived to interrogate the tiny witch. Together, they heard her confession. Tearfully, she held out a forefinger and told them where her "familiar," a little snake, used to suck, "where they observed a deep red spot, about the bigness of a flea bite" (which it probably was). Kept in jail for the next eight months, Dorcas would watch her suckling infant sister die and her mother led away to the gallows, cry her heart out, and go insane.

Summoned by the extemporaneous conversation between ministers on the pulpit and the girls in the pews that led to new accusations, the magistrates reappeared and resumed the interrogation of suspects. This time Hathorne and Corwin were troubled, for the accused were not outsiders or marginal members of the community like Osborn, Good, and Tituba but fully integrated participants in village and church life. The girls, however, had seized the chance to polish their performance. The stakes were higher, but the girls had found a corporate identity and new status in the community by bringing accusations, and they became the center of attention by acting them out. One would call out that she saw the specter of the supposed witch attacking another of the accusers, and the latter would cry out in pain. Their accusations played to packed houses. The cathartic effect was real, just as it was in Greek tragedy. The girls were never alone, never separated from each other, never examined in private. Thus they could engage in ensemble acting.

The examinations convened on a regular basis, the episodic quality of the first month's revelations becoming a continuous feature of Salem life. Seen for the first time, the hearings might have appeared to be disorderly affairs. In fact, they had a clear structure. The examiners, notably Hathorne, began to direct the girls' performance, prompting them into their fits by asking them to identify the suspects, cuing the girls to interject their own voices and act out in chorus their afflictions, demanding that the suspects touch the girls to alleviate their symptoms. The ministers present, always Parris and often John Hale, or Nicholas Noyse, from Salem Town, pressured the girls to reconsider their accusations but otherwise did not intervene, even when the accused was a longtime friend and congregant. As the web of accusations spun out beyond Corey and Nurse, to Sarah Cloyse and Mary Esty, Nurse's sisters, John and Elizabeth Proctor, and others in good standing in the church and the town, the magistrates no longer hesitated. The girls added new names to the list, and the magistrates brought all the accused to confront their accusers. And if no one could see what the girls said they saw—specters of the witches, the disembodied images of the accused swooping down upon the girls—the magistrates and the ministers believed what they did see.

The girls used props as well. Pins, normally worn to keep dresses and bonnets together, became instruments of torture, as the girls accused defendants of pricking them. Mary Black, a slave of Nathaniel Putnam, accused by Ann Putnam and others, was made at her examination on April 22, 1692, to repin her neck cloth in front of the girls. They then complained of being pricked. Mary Walcott was able to show Hathorne and Corwin where blood came from a prick mark on her arm. One can speculate that Mary Black was not the only one who brought pins to the examination. Witnesses for the defendants saw how the accusers used pins. Sarah Nurse caught Sarah Bibber, one of the older women who had joined the accusers, pulling pins out of her clothing, hiding them in her hands, pricking herself, then crying out against Rebecca Nurse. Bruises and bite marks were similarly produced and displayed.

So dramatic and so portentous were these events that the provisional deputy governor, Thomas Danforth, and four of the former assistants—

temporarily the governing council of the colony—traveled to Salem to witness the spectacle on April 11. They were not disappointed. The girls had found a new way to avoid bearing false witness. When asked who it was that afflicted them, they were struck dumb. Lewis's mouth was stopped; Putnam could not utter a word; Williams's fist was "thrust in her own mouth." Their silence became the accusation. Parris took notes as Cloyse and Elizabeth and John Proctor, his own parishioners, stood accused.

At first, Danforth frightened the girls, telling them that lying would be punished in another, higher court. Awed by his manner and his office, some of the girls backed away from earlier testimony that Cloyse and Proctor had come as specters and hurt them. In the middle of the examination, with Indian John showing his bruises and Ann Jr. and Abigail bawling, Proctor turned to the girls and admonished them gently but firmly, as she would her own children, that there was another, higher judgment, but Williams brazened out her earlier charges.

Danforth might have seen through the maze of contradictions and asserted his authority to quiet the crisis, but he faltered. Unsure whether to believe the girls' performance, but certain that the Devil was abroad and that witches were His agents, Danforth left the matter where it was. Another opportunity had been lost, but in fairness Danforth was not looking for such opportunities. He, more than the Villagers, knew that the entire colony was in peril from the French and Indians to the north and west and the politicians in England. The five men returned to Boston.

The tidal wave of accusations overwhelmed the institutions of criminal justice that had, until now, served the colony adequately. The purpose of a criminal justice system is to process those accused of crime. The key elements of Massachusetts's criminal procedure—speed, inexpensiveness, and social control—simply were unsuited to unmasking falsity on such a scale. The Massachusetts criminal courts, except in notorious cases, prodded the accused to accept guilt and then arranged for some punishment that permitted the accused to reinstate herself in the social web. Thus, until 1692, most accusations of witchcraft had failed to lead to conviction, even when neighbors complained about the defendant for many years. Magistrates required the suspect to conform more closely to the expectations of neighborliness and quieted, at least for a time, the community's fears.

Salem's trials did not perform this function—in fact, the reverse was true. Hunted in their homes, the faces of their neighbors turned against them, confined to jail in conditions that were degrading and unhealthy, and unable to sway the girls' testimony, suspects began to confess to crimes they had not committed. The first had been Tituba. The next was Abigail Hobbs, on April 19. "I will speak the truth," she told the magistrates. "I have seen many sights and been scared. I have been very wicked. I hope I shall be better, if God will help me." Hobbs did not have the opportunity, like Tituba, to deliberately misunderstand and then reconfigure the magistrates' questions. She admitted she had seen the Devil. She reported their conversations. She described her familiars. She confessed to pinching little Ann Putnam and Lewis at the Devil's command. The next day, she identified Sarah Good as another witch and described how she had eaten the red bread and wine at a "witches' Sabbath" in Parris's pasture. It was nonsense, and she knew it, but she had become an informer and could not stop. Her immediate safety depended upon her testimony.

The more the magistrates heard that confirmed the work of the Devil, the more skeptical of contradictory evidence they became. It is a classic example of avoiding cognitive dissonance. Evidence that did not fit was discarded or attacked; evidence consistent with the assumption of a widespread conspiracy was believed and integrated into the story. The magistrates' dogged resistance to inconsistency and recantation rested upon more than their aversion to dissonance, however. They shared the larger psychology of Puritanism, a state of mental tension and unease. Election—salvation—lay wholly in the hands of God. No men or women could save themselves, though they might search penitently for signs of grace and order their steps upon the straight and narrow. In the gap between justification through God's unhindered grace and the orderly life every good Puritan was expected to lead, there lay days of worry and nights of yearning for signs that he or she was truly regenerate. The magistrates were not immune to the agonies of uncertainty about their own souls' state, and the stakes were raised by the witchcraft accusations. The Devil was abroad, and to be uncertain about His intentions was to lay open all of God's commonwealth to the Great Deceiver's evil plan. Their own religious convictions thrust upon Hathorne and Corwin the need to be sure, certain, unwavering, and right.

Thus even those accounts that defied common experience, like witches holding midnight Sabbaths in open fields to which they flew on poles, were credited, for the alternative was to abandon the entire structure of belief and testimony. There was no way to limit credulity. Of course, witchcraft itself defied common experience, and some of the most popular learned writers of treatises on witchcraft admitted that the Devil might empower women to assume the shapes of animals or go from house to house in spectral form. The greater the stress on them to find the truth, the more the magistrates clung to what they had been told.

On May 14, help for the beleaguered people of Salem arrived in the person of the newly appointed governor, William Phips, returned from England with a revised charter and the power to do something about the crisis. As Cotton Mather, one of Phips's great admirers, later wrote with characteristic hyperbole, "Sir William Phips, at last being dropt, as it were, from the Machine of Heaven, was an instrument for easing the distresses of the land." Phips was a professional sailor, merchant, courtier, and warrior, a tough and plainspoken man who had risen from life on the Maine frontier to a place at the side of kings. He was not learned in theology or law, and he had other problems on his mind than witches. He was beset by those in the antiroyal party who did not want his mission in New England to succeed. The witchcraft scandal made him look bad. The new charter he brought was itself untested, and the control over the government it gave to the king was disquieting to many Puritans. Meanwhile, the jails were filling, and the colony teetered on the brink of chaos. Phips had to do something fast, and he did.

CHAPTER 6

The Judges, the Ministers, and the Law

Phips created a special court to handle the witchcraft crisis, a court of oyer and terminer—literally, in the "law French" that was the second tongue of English law, to "hear and determine" the cases. Such courts were common in the colonies. Had the Salem cases arisen before 1691, they would have been heard in the old Court of Assistants. Never had the Assistants had to face an epidemic of such virulence as Phips and his new council now confronted, however. He could have waited for the new legislature to meet and pass a law creating a high court, and then have submitted the law along with his nominees for the new court's bench to the king for approval. But the contagion would have run wild in the meantime, and if it did, Phips might not have remained in office long enough to see the results of the cautious approach bear fruit. Far away in England, John Evelyn pierced to the heart of the matter, noting in his diary "unheard of stories of the universal increase of witches in New England; men, women, and children devoting themselves to the Devil so as to threaten the subversion of government." Phips could not have put it better.

He said as much in the commission for the new court he issued on May 27. He began, "[T]here are many criminal offenders now in custody" (presumably guilty, else they were not offenders—after all, no one had been tried yet), against whom the commissioners were to hear and determine "all manner of crimes and offenses." The judges were to act "according to the law and custom of England and of this their Majesties' Province," a command dictated by the new charter and somewhat disingenuously (or perhaps just negligently, for Phips was no lawyer) ignoring the difference between the laws of the two jurisdictions. Phips delegated authority to a number of his councillors to sit as judges and resolve the matter expeditiously. He was a military man and wanted action, having little use by temperament or training for delicate compromise, much less deliberation, and none for the nice-ties of legal procedure. For him, the real problem was that there were "many inconveniences attending the thronging of the jails [by suspects] at this hot season of the year." The prisoners might die of disease or, worse, might break out en masse. Either way, his reputation and good order in the colony were at stake.

Of the judges he named to the new court, Chief Judge William Stoughton, John Richards, Wait Winthrop, and Samuel Sewall had been judges of the Court of Assistants that met under the old charter. It was natural for Phips to turn to those who had judicial experience and were closest to him, and he was not bothered by the fact that the judges were also members of his council (in effect the upper legisla-tive chamber of the colony). There was no bar to holding multiple offices in the American colonies. In addition, Stoughton was the lieu-tenant governor of the colony.

Stoughton would be the most important judge at the trials. He had gone to Harvard College to be a minister but had never really felt the calling and had turned to politics instead. An unattractive character but an astute manager of his own affairs, Stoughton was a land specu-lator and defrauder of the Indians. His political ambitions were well known, and his skills in political infighting superbly honed. He had gone to England to lobby for the colony against revocation of its old charter, changed sides to serve his political ally Joseph Dudley after the charter was revoked, remained a judge under much hated royal governor Edmund Andros while managing to convince most of his countrymen that he still favored their interests over the Crown's, and then landed on his feet like a cat when Andros was jailed and his government overturned in 1689. When Phips was recalled in 1694, Stoughton would succeed him as governor. Years later Stoughton re-mained convinced that he had done right by God and country in his conduct of the trials. A portrait of him done late in life shows a dour, long-faced man, his features doughy and slack.

Returning to Salem from Boston with Stoughton was Bartholomew Gedney, a Salem physician and merchant, and an old cohort of the chief judge. They had sat together on Dudley's short-lived council, along with Hathorne, when the old charter was revoked. Unpopular for a time in Salem, Gedney and Hathorne nevertheless sniffed the wind and joined in the rebellion against Andros in time to be reinstated in power under the new charter. Stoughton, Gedney, and Hathorne were thus veteran politicians and, perhaps even more important, canny survivors.

Corwin would sit on the bench after the June 2 trials, but he was the last judge from Salem. The others were not Salem men. The most prominent of these outsiders was Connecticut born and bred Wait Winthrop, grandson of Massachusetts's governor John Winthrop and son of Connecticut's governor John Winthrop Jr. Unfortunately, Wait lacked the moderation of his father and the statesmanship of his grandfather. The youngest Winthrop spent most of his time feuding with his in-laws over the division of his father's real estate, dabbling in commercial ventures, and seeking political office, which he managed to hold under the old charter, the Dominion, and after the ouster of Andros. His real skills lay largely in the area of self-promotion and sycophancy. From Boston also came Peter Sergeant and John Richards, merchants, leaders of the mercantile party there, and supporters of Phips. Richards had joined Stoughton in Dudley's government and, with Winthrop and Stoughton, had sat on the Court of Assistants.

Richards, Stoughton, and Winthrop were close personal friends of Cotton Mather and members of his church. Mather had dedicated his book on omens and prodigies, *Memorable Providences,* to Winthrop, with the confidence that "Your knowledge has qualified you to make those reflections on the following relations, which few can think, and this not fit that all should see." Stoughton had watched with near-paternal pride (for the lieutenant governor was a bachelor) the progress of young Mather.

The other members of the court were less closely associated with the Mathers but had long experience with the courts in the colony. Nathaniel Saltonstall was a farmer-soldier from Haverhill whose fairness and leniency had made him a perennial choice for the Assistants and later the council. He served as a justice of the peace for Essex County and on occasion sat on the quarterly courts in Salem. After the first trial, he left the court and had no more to do with the trials. Samuel Sewall, a Boston merchant whose diary reveals him as a man of profound sensibility and good sense, also was troubled by the trials. He had gone to Harvard with George Burroughs and counted him a friend, but Sewall was a man of traditional beliefs. He had no doubt that there was witchcraft abroad, and he sat on the court of oyer and terminer through the summer without recording in his diary or letters any dismay over the conduct of the trials. Five years later he made public confession of his credulity.

The judges were men of experience but not bred to the law. More important, much of their experience derived from a time when Massachusetts had its own charter and more or less made its own laws. These conformed to but did not duplicate the laws of England, and the colony's lawmakers gloried in their autonomy. By the late spring of 1692, however, when the Puritan authorities had most need of the old certainties, the document upon which these truths rested, the first charter, had been gone for nearly a decade, and the new charter was not yet tested. The lawmaking body, still styled the General Court, had not yet met, and there were no regular courts—hence the need for a special court to try suspected witches. The uncertain basis of Massachusetts criminal law and courts seemed to some to leave an opening wedge for the Devil and His minions to do their mischief. Was the Devil seizing the moment to overthrow God's commonwealth?

The new charter told Phips's judges to conform to English law, but even if they wanted to comply, there were no hard-and-fast rules of evidence in English law. Formal rules of evidence in criminal trials had not yet evolved by 1692 and would not for many years to come. The basic notion of empirical measurement of truth by reasonable observers was gaining support in English educated circles and beginning to cross over into English criminal law by the end of the seventeenth century, but juries in England were still treated to a mixture of rumor, supposition, lies, tall tales, and personal spite. Massachusetts law under the first charter had standards for legal proof, but these were vague to the point of uselessness. Proof was to be "convincing and sufficient," but the rules as written did not distinguish between conviction as a psychological state and conviction as a matter of moral certainty.

The best evidence of crime is probative—it proves to the jury that the facts are as alleged. Probative evidence may be direct (that is, eyewitness testimony) or indirect (recreated through a convincing sequence of circumstantial inferences). The worst evidence is mere prejudice, which induces a jury to reach a verdict on an improper basis. Witchcraft cases threw these precepts into the wastebasket, for witchcraft was a hidden crime. Who but another witch might know that the suspect had struck a pact with the Devil or guess that the strange animal in the lane or the loft was a witch's familiar? Only perpetrators' or confederates' confessions could establish that a pact with the Devil existed (no one else saw Him), but such confessions themselves might have been induced by duress or fear, as they had in Salem. Thus witchcraft cases relied on indirect evidence, more often than not evidence which only victims could see. Such testimony as the girls of Salem gave might easily prejudice a jury, and defendants could not refute the girls' assertions because no one else could observe what the accusers swore they saw.

Once upon a time in earlier English history, the trial jury determined the verdict based upon its own knowledge of the events. In effect, the jury generated the evidence. By the 1690s this method had been fully replaced by the notion that the jurors were to hear and see the evidence presented at trial and, weighing that alone, putting aside their own pre-existing conceptions, reach a finding of fact. Hearsay, which cannot be admitted in a modern criminal proceeding except in special circumstances, was perfectly fair game in these trials. In general, judges could allow into evidence a wide array of assertions, tales, surmises, and gossip—or they could exclude or discount it.

Judges could also instruct juries on how they were to weigh any piece of evidence but could not tell juries what they must believe. A juror's "conviction" depended not on a judge's ruling but on the cognitive structures of that juror's mind. Judges usually instructed seventeenth-century jurors to look to their consciences, for conscience was not only a moral faculty but also a way of sifting truth from falsehood. A "safe conscience" meant a discerning intelligence, and witchcraft presented special problems for even the most informed conscience. Jurors needed help that went beyond legal rulings—they needed to know what was real and what imagined, what they could trust and what they ought to disregard.

For help in instructing jurors about the invisible world, the judges looked to the ministers. There was nothing surprising or illicit in the judges' turning to ministers for help. Today, we have erected a wall between church and state, in part to protect religion from government interference, in part to protect the government from religious factionalism. Law and religion kept company in Puritan Massachusetts, although by the 1690s the companionship had grown quarrelsome. Religion depended upon faith, which for Puritans was all-encompassing, but religion was established in the colony not by faith but by law. With the demise of the original charter in 1684 through a legal process in the king's courts, the law that mandated Puritan belief was rescinded. After the Toleration Act of 1689 in England, Anglicans, Quakers, and other disrupters of Puritan hegemony could no longer be contained in New England.

Yet even as it threatened to topple the reign of the saints, law could never make itself independent of religion in Massachusetts. Even in the years without a charter, the law in practice (as opposed to the law on the books in England) rested upon the older religious ideal of a covenanted community. This godly law was embodied in codes of governance Massachusetts settlers had written for themselves, and its strictures persisted in people's minds. The criminal codes fashioned in 1641 and 1648 made biblical offenses like blasphemy and disobedience to parents into capital crimes. It is not clear whether anyone was ever executed for these offenses, but they exhorted everyone to stay within the boundaries of good conduct. Whether English or biblical in origin, criminal law drew lines in the earth that men and women crossed at their peril.

The close tie between ministerial and magisterial roles in New England also made the judges' recourse to the ministers a natural step. Church courts were an alternative to criminal courts for many misdemeanors. The ministry was highly politicized, as it had been since the founding of the colony, making leading clergymen into an informal network of political advisers. Ministers, including Cotton Mather, had played a hand in the ouster of Andros. Finally, the ministers were more than preachers and pastors. They were men of finely tuned and well-read intellects in a time when moral judgment and natural truths were not severed from each other. Together, the judges and ministers set out to tell jurors what evidence to credit.

When it came to catching witches, these men of learning had competition in Massachusetts, just as their counterparts had in England. Judges and ministers had to warn prospective jurors that "country people" were easily deceived by false conjurers and tricksters. Wise folks should shun the cunning man and the wizard, for they were witches themselves. The private witchfinder, like Caleb Powell in Newbury and Matthew Hopkins in England, who would "defame ten that are innocent before he discover one that is guilty," was thereby almost as dangerous as the witches he hunted. Cotton and Increase Mather agreed that the "illiterate" masses needed a guide and that such guide must be "learned, very learned." Discovering witches must be left "to the power of the magistracy and the ministry."

Late in May, Judge John Richards asked his minister, Cotton Mather, what to make of the evidence. Cotton Mather already felt the hot, angry breath of Satan brushing over his sleeve. Early in the crisis he warned his countrymen that "an Army of Devils is horribly broke in upon the place which is our center," and he vowed to stride forth against the foe armed with the shield of righteousness and the sword of good works. In 1688 he had sniffed the sulfuric approach of the Evil One in the suffering of the Goodwin boys and girls. By 1692 Mather detected that the Devil had turned His attention even closer to home: "And I myself expect not few or small buffetings from Evil Spirits." In Cotton Mather's works, folk beliefs and polite learning came together. Mather was a believer in the invisible world, the world of amazing events that opened a window into God's purposes. With a mixture of arrogant carelessness and true faith, Mather aspired to bridge the gap between the popular and the elite across the span of miraculous prodigies. In 1692 he was poised to speak for the rulers to the people and for the people to their rulers.

At the opening of the year, he searched the heavens and the earth for a "miraculous thing" to report to his diary. The appearance of devilish acts in Salem confirmed Mather's worst fears. Asked to attend the trials, Mather demurred. His health would not permit travel. He did offer to take some of the girls into his own home, as he did with the Goodwin children. This might have been a mark of his skepticism about their fits. A good observer, he needed to see for himself before he decided. At the same time, the offer evidenced a self-centeredness, an exaggerated belief in his own centrality to these events, that would bend out of shape the rest of his involvement in them. Though he would not attend, he wrote a letter to Judge Richards summarizing what previous generations of English clerics and jurists believed about proof of witchcraft. In treatises and tracts, charges to grand juries and philosophical lectures, these Englishmen had debated "cases of conscience" wherein men and women stood accused of witchcraft. Mather, a bibliophile, had read them all.

Cotton Mather's basic source was the work of William Perkins, the greatest Puritan student of these "cases of conscience." Perkins had written almost a hundred years before that jurymen must be very cautious in crediting what they heard at trial. True, there were certain "presumptions" that could be weighed against a defendant in a witchcraft inquiry. Among these were a notorious reputation, although ill fame might be no more than slander. The confession of fellow witches had to be taken seriously, but it was not sufficient, for it too might be motivated by malice. Curses followed by the illness of the person cursed were important signs, as were quarrels that seemed to precede mysterious maladies. If the suspect was a relative of a known witch, the matter was to be noted. The magistrate might look for a "Devil's mark," but such a mark was not proof of anything. If the suspect contradicted herself, she might have a guilty conscience, and that was a serious matter as well, but not a proof of guilt.

Such "presumptions" as Perkins made were based on contemporary notions of what the natural—and the unnatural—world was like. In the late sixteenth century, many educated men assumed that there was a spirit (invisible) world, and that the Devil and His witches could move freely through it. There could thus be a kind of magical causation that existed alongside ordinary, visible, material cause and effect. For a person reading Perkins in the 1590s, it was easy to accept the proposition that a quarrel, followed by an illness, might betoken a cause-and-effect relationship. To read Perkins in the 1690s with these same notions of empirical causation was another matter. Concepts of probability, rationality, and causation had greatly changed in the passing of a century, as Mather, himself an amateur scientist and an avid reader of works of science, well knew. Of course, the triumph of science over the supernatural was hardly complete in 1692, and in the absence of uncontested authority, Cotton Mather was free to believe that spectral evidence was valid rather than to reject it.

Mather elected to straddle the controversy rather than resolve it. He wrote, "[Y]ou do not lay more stress upon specter testimony than it will bear. When you are satisfied or have good, plain, legal evidence that the demons which molest our poor neighbors do indeed represent such and such people to the sufferers, tho' this be a presumption, yet I suppose you will not reckon it a condition that the people so represented are witches to be immediately exterminated." Mather conceded that Devils could choose the shapes of innocent people to do their mischief, just as Sarah Osborn and others had pleaded at their examinations a little over two months before. The accused might be "malignant, envious, malicious," and thereby might open their souls to the Devil's importunities, but if the court relied entirely on purely spectral evidence, that is, the victims' claiming to see a vision of the defendant in spectral form, no one would be safe from such accusations. At the same time, Mather was convinced that in Salem "a horrible witchcraft" had been uncovered and that many innocents suffered from the witches' activities. "The effects are dreadfully real," and the cause of them was "a capital crime."

Mather fretted, "Our neighbors at Salem are blown up after a sort, with an infernal gunpowder, under the floor." What could that mean? To us the reference may be obscure, but to his fellow Puritans the implication was obvious. In 1605 a band of Roman Catholics, driven to despair by King James's persecution of their faith, tried to blow up the English houses of Parliament. The plan was discovered at the last minute, and the conspirators were executed, but the "gunpowder plot" became a symbol among Protestants of the danger Roman Catholicism posed to English Protestantism. In 1689 Parliament drove James II, a Roman Catholic, from the throne of England and replaced him with a Dutch Protestant, William of Orange, and James's daughter, Mary, William's wife. They were to rule jointly. A war followed in which Protestants battled Roman Catholics at home and abroad. This was the war that brought the Indians and their French Roman Catholic allies to the doorstep of Salem. Thus the Puritans saw Roman Catholicism as a continuing and powerful threat to Protestantism in England and the survival of Puritanism in New England. They also believed that Roman Catholic priests were in league with the Devil. Reports of priests and Indians worshiping the Devil before they attacked Massachusetts towns regularly made the rounds of the colony.

But the problem of spectral evidence remained, for the only ones who could see the witches in their spectral form, and thus say who it was that caused their pain, were the accusers themselves. Here Mather could find no answers in his library. He must leave it and enter the world of ordinary people. No abstract theory or abstruse theology could dictate commonly accepted contemporary notions of the truth of testimony. The parallel to children's evidence in child abuse cases is again striking and informative. Modern authorities, at least until quite recently, tended to believe what children said in cases of suspected sexual abuse because the authorities could not accept the possibility that children could make up such stories. In recent years such a conclusion has been challenged. Children—even very young children—are so tutored in the danger signs of abuse that they know how to fashion a plausible accusation, just as girls in Salem knew enough about witchcraft to fake the symptoms. Mather had seen the suffering of children—his own and others'. He knew how suddenly and senselessly death could come to the young, as it had to all but one of his children. He was thus disposed to believe the girls.

Despite Cotton Mather's desire to help the girls, he could not bring himself to rely upon popular beliefs—for that would not be "very learned." There had to be some legal authority upon which to base a learned opinion, and he found it in the works of one of England's foremost judges. Chief Justice Matthew Hale's trial of accused witches at Bury St. Edmunds in 1664 supported Mather's view of spectral evidence. Mather's version of the account, dated 1682, reported the suffering of the two Durent children and others at the hands of Rose Cullender and Amy Duny. When the girls took sick, a doctor advised their mother to hang the children's blanket in the chimney corner all day and to shake it out at night. Plainly this was a form of countermagic, for the good doctor was convinced that the girls' fits could not have a natural cause. When the mother shook out the blanket, a toad fell to the floor, which the girls' brother burned in the fire. Duny was in pain the next day. Soon the girls' fits worsened, however, and they saw specters of the witches. In court they renewed their fits and pointed to the spectral forms of the defendants. They vomited pins and convulsed themselves, and only the death of the accused ended the children's misery. Then they recovered completely. Hale instructed the jury that spectral evidence was acceptable. That Hale's view was disputed at the time—indeed, at the very same moment he was crediting spectral evidence, his fellow judges at the Somerset Assizes were dismissing it—might have swayed a trained jurist from citing Hale. Indeed, Hale himself, some years later, seemed to back away from his views of spectral evidence. But these considerations did not deter Mather.

In the end, Mather decided that a confession was the best evidence. Had not some of the witches already confessed? In other countries such confessions were regarded by inquisitors with derision or incredulity—the confessors must be deranged or liars—but in England and New England confessions remained proof of complicity, as Increase Mather reported in his *Illustrious Providences* (1684): "It is a vain thing, for the patrons of witches to think they can sham of this argument, by suggesting that these confessions did proceed from the deluded imaginations of mad and melancholy persons." Although some confessions were undoubtedly forced or foolish, others were not.

Moreover, Cotton Mather allowed that the suspected witches' words could be used against them even when the suspects denied being witches. He did not require that collaborators' testimony be corroborated in some way. That was a technical point, and he did not trace out the technical points of law. Mather even hinted that looking for Devil's marks and touching the accused to relieve the symptons, tests other Puritan and legal authorities explicitly ruled out, might be reintroduced when the circumstances were ripe, for Mather was certain in his heart that the Devil was behind the events in Salem. Cotton Mather read Perkins's caution and misstated it, reading it not in the light of Perkins's own text but in the light of necessity—in particular, the political crisis of the colony and the terrors of war. War against the Devil and war against the popish French and their Indian allies were the same in his mind. Caution played into the hands of the enemies of Cotton Mather's brand of Puritanism, and he urged Richards to credit what he heard. But in the first case he heard, Richards had another guide: reputation.

The Disreputable Woman

Bridget Bishop was tried and convicted for the crime of witchcraft on June 2, 1692. She was executed eight days later. Few lamented her passing, for she was a disputatious and troublesome woman.

In the Puritan world of New England, reputation was not so much a matter of honor and shame as of moral virtue and guilt. In part reputation was assigned to an individual by others, but in part it was generated by internal normative standards that everyone was expected to understand and adopt. A good name was based on one's conduct toward others. A good neighbor did not slander, gossip, or backbite. A good person accepted the vicissitudes of life without complaint. A good friend was grateful and shared others' burdens. And it was hard to be malicious without everyone else knowing, for there was little privacy in this world. Oddities of personality might be tolerated, but misconduct was routinely reported and immediately censured.

Visible piety was another characteristic of worthiness. Regular church attendance was valued, but the highest sign of religious virtue was the ability to stand before a congregation and narrate an experience of grace. Some congregations required that submission before they would admit a would-be worshiper to full membership. Those who were not full members of congregations were thus less worthy in the eyes of their neighbors.

Wealth was another gauge of virtue not because the rich were saved or because a well-to-do person could buy his or her way into Heaven but because wealth denoted good stewardship and self-discipline, qualities the Puritans appreciated. Even the wealthy offered apologies for their gains, lest others suspect that pursuit of profit had replaced pursuit of holiness in the apologizers' lives. In the meantime, affluence brought social status and bought the best pew in the meetinghouse. Riches even gave parents added control of their children, for children usually did not marry until they had some stake in the world, and parents with land and goods could prevent marriage (ensuring that the children continue to contribute their labor to the family business) for a longer time.

To be sure, there were special burdens for the good, the pious, and the wealthy. One of these was charity to the poor. Although the migration to New England in the 1630s and 1640s included able and skilled men and women, many of whom left established businesses, farms, and shops in England to find a new life, others on the ships were laborers, servants, and even ne'er-do-wells. The economic "improvement" that commerce brought to England in the sixteenth and early seventeenth centuries drove many poor farmers out of their cottages and onto the roads seeking work. Some became beggars or vagrants. Poor young men and women signed indentures to serve in New England. They were joined by weavers and spinners who could not make ends meet. When these transient laborers or their children could not maintain themselves, New England towns routinely "warned them out," but they merely relocated to another town. In the second and third generations of settlement, children of even the well-to-do emigrants sometimes failed to rise to their parents' economic level, adding to the numbers of poor.

For women, extremes of both poverty and property presented special problems. Women did not have the economic opportunities or the geographic mobility of men, so for them poverty was always just around the corner. Although Puritan theology and social ideas did not portray women as inherently sinful, the range of their public behavior was more limited than men's. What might be aggressive but permissible in men's economic activities was censured in women's. The law merged a married woman's property with her husband's and gave him control over it. Poverty in a woman was thus both more common and more suspect than poverty in a man. At the same time, property was a greater burden for women than for men. Single women and widows were not as limited by the law as married women, but women with property who were not married faced the envy of others in a way that single men did not. Relatives coveted the widow's portion, and unscrupulous single men eyed single women with estates as targets of exploitation.

At one time or another, Bridget Bishop of Salem had violated or transgressed almost all of these expectations of virtue in a woman. She had the reputation of dunning those who owed her money and dodging those she owed. She spoke ill of neighbors and harassed her enemies in public. Notoriously and defiantly, she had run through her first two husbands' estates and kept a house of ill repute with her doddering third husband's consent. Almost sixty years old in 1692, she had been accused of both witchcraft and theft in the 1680s and had walked away from the charges.

Again accused of witchcraft by the girls in late April, Bishop came to her examination with fire in her eyes. Unlike the other women, she challenged everyone in the room to admit that she was "clear" of the accusation. Indeed, they agreed that she had never come into the Village, but her reputation had flown down its pathways, and the girls had no trouble describing her witchery. Dogged by Hathorne, she tried to stare him and the girls down, an extremely aggressive act, given the fear that everyone had of the witch's "evil eye." Thomas Newton, the first special prosecutor Phips chose for the trials, had no trouble deciding whom to prosecute when the trials began: Bridget Bishop, that disreputable woman.

The first trial's date was set for June 2. To Salem came the judges. Salem in the late spring: mud turning to dust; wet, cold nights becoming humid and sultry; and now witchcraft everywhere. The people who gathered in the town waiting for the trials to begin looked at neighbors' faces and wondered if familiar features hid Devil's marks. The judges, most of them from out of town, surrounded by unruly and apprehensive crowds, nervously returned the stares of the onlookers. The judges might become victims of the witches themselves (for virtue was no shield against Satan's malignity), and this added to the judges' desire to have done with the business once and for all.

To Salem also came a procession of witnesses and suspects, less three of the principal actors. Tituba, caged first in Salem, was sent to Boston jail and finally cleared by an Ipswich grand jury on May 9. Her confession had not saved her, for no other confessor was released. The grand jury simply refused to believe her. Throughout the spring and summer trials she was incarcerated, however, for even the innocent had to pay the "costs" of incarceration, and her master, Samuel Parris, would not put up the money. Finally, she was sold to another man to pay for her imprisonment. Betty was hidden away in Stephen Sewall's house, around the corner on Main Street from the two-story courthouse. Cotton Mather's influence hovered over the proceedings, but he was too ill to attend the trials until August.

For most of the parties, the shift in setting was dramatic—no longer the farms and marshes, the rocky fenced fields and dirt roads of the Village. Whole families of Villagers flowed to Salem down the Andover and Ipswich roads; down the hill through what is now the town of Peabody went the witnesses and the accused. Thomas Putnam and his two Anns had to travel the farthest of any of the Villagers, from the northwestern extremity of the settlement, five and a half miles as the crow flies. Bridget Bishop had once lived at the edge of the North River, just a few houses away from the courthouse. Now she lived on the Ipswich road, but her journey was still one of the shortest.

Other suspects were already in jail in Boston or Salem, missing the end of the spring planting season in their fields to sit in the heat and dust of the second-floor courthouse. Bound and taken by the sheriffs or the constables, they had passed down Main Street (now Essex Street), past the corner of Summer Street, where Judge Corwin lived in well-furnished elegance (in what is now locally titled the "witch house"), and past Stephen Sewall's house, then turned north up Prison Lane to the Salem jail. They had traveled this route before, to bring their goods to market or to buy from Salem storekeepers, even to worship in the Salem church, then under repair. This trip was different and full of dread.

Yet there was to be no inquisition. Defendants were given their "day" wherein they could speak for themselves, call witnesses, cross-examine the accusers, and produce evidence of their innocence. Defendants and their witnesses could not testify on oath, however, although prosecution witnesses did. In a criminal justice system dependent upon the sacredness of oath taking and oath giving, the defendant was at a disadvantage. A grand jury had to indict before the trial, and a trial jury convict the defendant, but the average criminal trial took less than an hour and in reality amounted to little more than an altercation in front of a judge and trial jury.

As soon as they convened the court, the judges called the grand jury and submitted to it evidence regarding all those men and women in custody. A day was set aside for grand jury hearings. The records of the spring and summer 1692 trials are lost, but at the January 1693 trials, for which the records survive, two grand jurors from the nearby towns were chosen either by town constables or by town meetings. The grand jury was a relic of much older English criminal procedure and once presented suspects to the king's justices upon the knowledge of the jurors. Grand juries still performed this function in New England, presenting fornicators, nonchurchgoers, and other minor miscreants based on the grand jurors' own information. In a suspected felony, that is, serious crimes whose punishments might mean loss of life or limb, grand juries merely certified whether there seemed probable cause to hold the suspect for a trial. The suspect then might plea-bargain for a lesser charge, confessing to it whether he or she was guilty or not. That is in effect what some of the suspected witches tried to do with their confessions, a far better explanation of their accounts of flying through the air and seeing men change into animals than hysteria or some other psychological or spiritual experience. Until 1692 such confessions availed little, but the accused had learned (again, the oral networks superseding the book law) that confession would lead to a happier result on this occasion. In fact no one who confessed, and many did, was executed, unless they recanted the confession.

In the first round of indictments, stretching over the spring and summer of 1692, the grand juries exercised a good deal of independent judgment. They did not rubber-stamp the bills of indictment the magistrates drew up. Instead, despite the professions and physical demonstrations by the girls, without confirmation from other, more traditional, sources, the grand jury would not indict a suspect. For the grand juries, spectral evidence, in the form of the girls' assertions, was not enough, even when it was featured in the examinations of the suspects. The grand jurors were not proof against the power of rumor, however, and panic rumors had driven the first prosecutions. It was only when these rumors died down—when the first panic had abated and the Devil had not shown His own face—that grand jurors started to openly doubt what they heard. Also, although nearly half of the defendants were related to one another, by marriage or blood (this was common in England as well), grand juries did not unreflectingly indict everyone in a suspect family. More often than not, only one or two of the adult women would be indicted. Grand jurors simply refused to believe that witchcraft corrupted entire families.

In the trials that occurred in 1693, trial jurors were selected from the towns, but we do not know how many towns were asked to provide jurors for the trials in 1692. We can be sure that there was always more than one panel of trial jurors, for a defendant had the right to object to jurors "for just and reasonable cause." On the second day the court sat to hear trial on those "true bills" (indictments) by the grand jurors. The trial jury was called, sworn, and seated. The defendant was brought forward and either accepted the jury or made her objections. Once the final panel was chosen, the indictments were recited. These were followed by written evidence read aloud. Oral examination and the defendant's case ensued. The jury then retired, discussed its verdict, returned, and gave it. The verdict had to be unanimous. Perplexed, members of a jury might seek the aid of the bench by rendering a "special verdict" (allowing the judge to decide whether the jurors' finding of a particular set of facts amounted to any particular crime) or by giving a partial verdict (guilty of A but not of B). They might even seek the aid of those in the courtroom.

The trial jury was supposed to sift through the words of the many parties and arrive at a verdict based on facts. Thus even for the most heinous of crimes, juries did not always convict the defendant. Instead, in most cases one had slightly less than a fifty-fifty chance of getting off. In witchcraft cases, however, instead of acting as finders of fact, the trial juries in Salem put the community seal of approval upon the judges' decision to admit spectral evidence. Everyone who came to trial was convicted, an unheard-of rate for Massachusetts then, before, or later. Unlike the grand jurors, who gathered themselves apart from the judges, the jurors had to see and hear the bench, and the judges could see the jurors' faces. To have opposed the bench when chief judge Stoughton so obviously wanted to convict the accused would have taken an act of considerable courage.

Or the jurors may have believed the accusers for the same reason as the judges and the ministers, at least at first. Everyone believed in witches, feared Satan, and was appalled and convinced by the girls' testimony—that is, so long as the girls were permitted to testify to the "maleficium" of apparitions. Once the central fact—that the girls were bewitched—was established beyond dispute, the jurors could lay aside their qualms about spectral evidence. The judges' decision to admit spectral evidence thus reinforced the jurors' preexisting belief rather than commanding the jurors to credit what had hitherto seemed improbable to them. At trial, the language that the jury heard, guided by the implicit and explicit instructions of the judges—that is, the cues the judges gave by their questions, their visual signals, and their willingness to admit all manner of hearsay—then enabled popular belief to run free. And throughout the proceedings, Stoughton and his brethren indulged popular imagination.

But juries could have resisted. At the local level, the administration of the criminal law was a bargain between local juries and central authority. The power of the state was represented by the bench, but it had to have the cooperation of the defendants' neighbors to penalize anyone. In England and New England, criminal trial juries did not content themselves with obeying instructions. They often bent the law or adjusted the facts to arrive at what they thought was a just outcome. True, by the end of the seventeenth century, such jury "nullification" of book law in criminal cases almost always had the tacit consent of the judges. For example, when a young person was accused of a capital offense like grand larceny (taking something worth more than one shilling), juries were known to "mitigate" the offense—that is, fully recognizing that the defendant was guilty as charged, nevertheless enter into a complex bargaining situation with the judge, and sometimes the victim, to reduce the severity of the offense. Ordinarily, the jury announced that the defendant was guilty of stealing eleven pence worth—one penny less than the one-shilling minimum for grand larceny. The offense thus became petty larceny, and the youthful offender got off with a lesser sentence. In effect, the jury was brokering a variation of the charge, not changing the law or making law but moving the defendant from one legal category to a lesser one.

In Massachusetts witchcraft trials, however, juries were not sources of leniency. They did not bargain with the judges to reduce the charges or alter the facts to mitigate the lawfully prescribed penalty. They might find, as they did on a few occasions, that the defendant was not guilty of witchcraft "under the law," but in these cases the jurymen were only following the judges' instructions. On a few occasions, the judges reversed or held in abeyance a jury's guilty verdict upon the judges' own reluctance to convict given the evidence presented in court. But we can be certain that judges in Salem did not signal juries that the bench would be amenable to jury mitigation.

As important as the two kinds of juries were in these cases, the judges had more to say about the outcome of the trials than anyone else. Their place—the bench—was raised and at the front of the courtroom, and everyone could hear what they uttered. Their voices were loud, literally and figuratively, for on occasion they had to shout over the noise of the assemblage. One would guess that the most imposing and most authoritarian figure on the bench, Chief Judge Stoughton, dominated the proceedings. From the one or two accounts we have from those present, he is the only judge whose name was mentioned. Later reports by Cotton Mather, Stoughton's friend and supporter, and Mather's chief critic, Boston merchant Robert Calef, ironically agree that Stoughton was a moving force behind the bench. Stoughton and his brethren did much of the questioning and spoke more frequently than anyone else. That was the custom in Massachusetts and English courts, but the custom had different repercussions in the two places.

In England the preeminence of the judge's voice in criminal trials was a tribute to the status of the judges. They not only represented the king's person in his courts but also were learned men, respected throughout the legal profession. In Salem the bench was experienced, but none of the judges were respected jurists. These may have been, as some scholars argue, a group of able men, but they were not lawyers, and no law was cited or debated in the court. Instead, folk witch-finding techniques like the touching test and examination for Devil's marks were allowed.

Politics combined with the relative lack of juridical sophistication to press the judges toward a sanguinary stance. The English high court judge, though a political appointee (he served at the pleasure of the Crown and was always aware of the Crown's displeasure), was not always a politician. Stoughton and the others on the court of oyer and terminer were first and foremost men on the make. It might have seemed to them that convictions in these cases would shore up the new government (or, in Stoughton's mind, further his own ambitions).

The pro-prosecutorial stance of the judges might have been deflected by legal counsel for the defendants, but no lawyers stepped forward during the trials to help the accused. Although the Massachusetts Body of Liberties had implied that defendants had a right to counsel, the Body of Liberties was gone. Massachusetts did not permit lawyers to practice for fees until 1705. Counsel was not allowed accused felons in England until 1836 (except in treason, and that in 1696), although by the eighteenth century, first in the colonies and later in England, counsel for the defense did appear in a small portion of the total number of cases. Their sharp words and quick wits, their colloquies with the judges, and their caustic, sometimes brutal, examination of witnesses built a recognizably modern trial procedure. If absence of counsel was not unusual, its effect was particularly harsh in the witchcraft trials, for counsel for the accused could cross-examine witnesses, finding loopholes and contradictions in their stories or malice in their motives. Counsel might have informed the judges of the outcomes of contemporaneous English trials. Such counsel become part of a judge's audience, and judges are often influenced by them or seek their aid. (Of course, the girls would probably have accused the lawyers of witchcraft before long.)

In Salem, the case against the defendant was presented by a special prosecutor. Thomas Newton, the first crown prosecutor Phips appointed, had experience in a highly charged political case not three years before. Newton had presented the crown case against Jacob Leisler, who had accomplished in New York what a number of the judges sitting in Salem had done in Massachusetts—overthrow a royal government—but Leisler would not relinquish power to King William's appointees. Leisler was hanged. At thirty-two, Newton expected that a long and prosperous career lay ahead for the man who swiftly drove the Devil out of Salem. Newton was replaced on July 27 by Anthony Checkley, the newly appointed attorney general of the colony. He was an experienced Salem lawyer (he represented Corwin, among others, in court) but no jurist.

Before their trials later in the summer, Mary Esty and Sarah Cloyse asked the judges to intervene for them and "direct us wherein we stand in neede." They conceded that they had no right to assistance from the bench but also knew that judges sometimes offered it to defendants, though only upon their own discretion and only to remedy errors in law. In state trials—trials that were politically important to the authorities—judges rarely interceded for the defendants. Quite the reverse was usually the case, as judges went out of their way to aid the state's case. There is no evidence that the Salem judges either helped or refused to help defendants when they faltered, for these trials had become state trials.

So Bridget Bishop stood before the tribunal alone. As in any state trial, which the prosecution cannot afford to lose, the most notorious offender is the first presented to the jury. Bishop fit that description. As early as 1679, neighbors had suspected her of witchcraft. Wonn, a field hand, had seen her image in a barn, stealing eggs. When he approached, she vanished, to reappear, he later testified, as a mysterious black cat. No one came forward then or later to argue for her, but Wonn's testimony was not sufficient, for no one was harmed by Bishop or the cat. At her pretrial hearing in Salem she was contrary and diffident by turns. Hathorne had tried to trap her in a lie and succeeded. Accused of being a witch, she puffed, "I am innocent to a witch, I know not what a witch is." Hathorne pounced: "How do you know then that you are not a witch?" Bishop, who surely did know what a witch was, for she had been accused of it before, and everyone knew what witches were, fell back upon deafness: "I do not know what you say." When Hathorne pressed on that Bishop had been accused by confessed witches, she retorted, "I know nothing of it," and Hathorne again had caught her lying. The clerk read to her that "John Hutchinson and John Lewis in open court affirmed that they had told her." Hathorne crowed: "[W]hy look you, you are taken now in a flat lye." What could she say? She stood naked to her enemies, and they were legion.

As the trial came on the magistrates gathered an impressive array of affidavits to her malignity and misconduct. Confessed witches Deliverance Hobbs and Mary Warren deposed that Bishop was one of them. Samuel Grey and others swore that Bishop had visited them at night and tormented them. The Reverend Hale passed on hearsay from his parishioners (for Bishop lived on the border with the town of Beverly) that she was the cause of evil among them. A jury of matrons found an "excrescence of flesh . . . not usual in women" on Bishop's body—the Devil's mark.

The grand jury returned four indictments against Bishop for exercising "certain detestable arts called witchcrafts and sorceries" on Lewis, Williams, Hubbard, and Ann Putnam Jr. The indictments did not cite the earlier acts of suspected witchcraft, however, but only the spectral visitation of Bishop upon the girls as they testified against her at the April 19 hearings. Thus spectral evidence was crucial. More important, because the indictments cited only what everyone had seen, that is, the torment of the girls at the hearing itself, the "two witness" requirement for indictment for felonies was not violated. Witchcraft was no longer a secret crime.

At her trial Bishop pleaded not guilty, but again the girls testified that it was her specter that afflicted them. With this testimony admitted, the door was opened to all manner of invisible evidence, and once more Samuel Grey, John Cook, John Bly and his wife, Richard Coman, Samuel Shattuck, John Louder, William Stacy, and William Bly described in vivid detail to the jury how they came to believe that Bishop was behind the misfortunes that had befallen them over the years. The pattern was always the same: a quarrel with Bishop, followed by bad luck. Sometimes she appeared in spectral form to claim credit for her work. The pièce de résistance came during the trial itself: "As this woman was under a Guard, passing by the great and spacious Meeting-house of Salem, she gave a look towards the house, and immediately a daemon invisibly entering the Meeting-house, tore down a part of it." Evidence of the efficacy of the "touching test" performed at the hearings was read to the jury. Deliverance Hobbs, by this time clearly insane, testified as well—and why not? The judges allowed all of it to come before the jury, and the jury was convinced. There was no delay; no respite; no time for Bishop to reconsider the state of her soul or to confess. Stoughton signed the death warrant without hesitation. Bishop was hanged in Salem on June 10.

Appalled by the conduct of the trial and wishing no more to do with the tribunal, Judge Saltonstall resigned. Corwin was named to replace him. Sewall kept his own counsel, but his minister in Boston, Samuel Willard, would not be muzzled and, with Saltonstall, may have contacted Phips. Phips had created the court and then gone off to fight the French and Indians in Maine. Dismayed at the news of dissent on the bench, he formally asked the ministers to report their thoughts to him and his council. Some of the ministers, including John Hale and Willard, had witnessed what happened at the first sitting of the court— the writhing of the girls and the absurd performance of Indian John, the reappearance of medieval forms of proof like the touching test, the absence of even the little bit of due process given suspected felons— and they recoiled. Mather had not traveled to Salem and could not dispute their account, nor did he wish to demean the honesty of their feelings. At the same time, they had not seen his letter to Richards, condoning in advance the very techniques they found revolting when the session was done.

The Ministerial Association met at Willard's insistence and asked Mather to prepare for their number a "Return of Several Ministers." On June 15 it issued forth. The "Return" retreated from Mather's own views and insisted that the court reduce the noise and openness of the trials. More important, no spectral evidence should be admitted, nor should the suspects be forced to touch the afflicted. The letter stopped short of condemning the outcome of the trial, however, and ended with a final paragraph that Mather had undoubtedly written on his own. On behalf of all thirteen signatories he urged "the speedy and vigorous prosecution of such as have rendered themselves obnoxious." All Cotton's life had led to this moment; all his aspirations and achievements were now bound in the few pages he sent on to Salem.

For the judges preparing for their second sitting, the issue was simpler than it was for the ministers. The latter had to reconcile science and theology, Bible and reason. The judges had only to decide whether spectral evidence should be admitted in court. The "Return of Several Ministers" said to stop using spectral evidence, but Mather was using a backstairs entry to the judge' chambers, and he supported the use of spectral evidence. The final paragraph, an amalgam of politics and presumptions, urged the judges to complete their work as they had begun it. Cotton Mather was an ally and admirer of Judge Stoughton, and he did not wish to injure or annoy him. Stoughton would later reply in kind with support for Mather's writings. No doubt at the time he signaled his approval of Mather's views. Cotton was already defensive about the effect of his earlier advice, a defensiveness stiffened by the criticism he sensed from the other signers, who had seen that the final paragraph went where they did not want it to go. Willard might have said something, for his opposition to the trial had become vocal since he signed the letter. Meanwhile, the judges continued to admit the girls' visions as evidence at trial.

Nevertheless, the conviction and execution of Bishop had led to the very situation that Phips had feared. The contagion spread. Andover, Beverly, Rowley, and Boston women and men had fallen under suspicion. There was no end in sight, and the judges were just getting started. Bishop was a troublemaker of long standing, but the next group of defendants included one woman whose reputation could not be so easily impeached. This was Goodwife Rebecca Nurse.

CHAPTER 8

The Good Wife

On June 29, 1692, Rebecca Nurse was tried and convicted of witchcraft. She was executed on July 19, mourned by many of her neighbors.

There were others like Bishop caught in the accusers' nets. They were women of ill repute or women who made themselves noisome and factious. There were women long suspected of practicing some form of the magic arts—an object of rumor for a long time and now an object of fear, like Susannah Martin. There were the cunning women whose cures failed to heal and whose animosity, reflected in the cold, hard faces of angry neighbors, became malignity. There were the old, whose enfeebled but determined grip on life now seemed to betoken some pact with the Devil. And there were women of valor, like Nurse.

Life expectancy in late-seventeenth-century England was but fifty years, less for a woman who faced the risk of death in childbirth or from postdelivery infection. The British West Indies were a graveyard for everyone, and the Chesapeake colonies were not much better. Few women survived there to see their grandchildren. But in New England, with care, luck, and good genes, a person might well survive into the seventh decade of life. Still, it was hard to be old and female in New England, for the winters were crueler on the old. The wet cold brought aching joints and made breathing difficult.

In ordinary circumstances to reach old age was something special. Not only had one found the secret of beating the odds but one had gained power. Oral societies, in which face-to-face contact was the norm for human interaction, made old people into respected elders. They were repositories of lore and custom, living libraries. This was especially true among all the Native American peoples. One of the reasons European diseases were so devastating to the Indians was that the diseases carried off the old and, with them, the village memory. The British also valued old age, revering the elders of the towns.

For the Puritans simple old age was not enough to guarantee respect. One had also to be pious. True, a pious life did not ensure salvation—that was in the hands of God according to the Calvinist doctrine of predestination that the Puritans adopted—but a good life and a pious life were synonymous and could be taken for a sign that God favored the individual. Puritans believed in such signs and recorded them in diaries, journals, and sermons.

Old Rebecca Nurse could boast of all these blessings. She was a full member in good standing of the church in Salem Village. She had done good works and with her husband had raised a family upright and strong. Occasionally, she had bursts of temper, as when she harangued Sarah and Benjamin Houlton for letting their pigs root through the Nurse garden. Benjamin died shortly thereafter, and his wife harbored suspicions that Nurse's anger had hastened the demise, but there was no reason to suspect witchcraft. As her neighbors attested, she had never done anything to suggest that she might be a witch. The Porters and some of the Putnams, notably John Sr. and Nathaniel, patriarchs of the family, agreed that Nurse was not a woman of ill fame. But she was vulnerable, for no one could be sure that a reputable woman like Nurse was not something else in private, a secret witch.

For the Puritans, secret unregeneracy was a long-standing theological and psychological problem. No one could tell God's plan or see into His mind. The saved were elected by Him and not by their own desire for grace or their life of good works. Even the most pious Puritans examined themselves daily for signs of their own secret unrepentance, for the mind was pliable and grace was never sure. There were so many temptations, and the Puritans refused to leave the everyday world to protect themselves against sin. Perfect faith was a guarantee of salvation, but who had that? Puritan diaries are full of longing for the safety of God's grace and full of fear that God had hidden His face from the diarist.

But the danger to Nurse came not from the debilities of her body or the weakness of her spirit. The danger came from without. First, it came from the girls, seeking additional witches. Nurse was not directly protected by the Porters. She had some property but was not a member of an elite family. There are hints in the records that she might have opposed the prosecutions if she had been left unaccused, and when she was named and examined, she proved that she did not fear them.

If the girls could pull her down, their power would be unstoppable. Danger also came from the younger Putnams, for Nurse was by birth and family connection a Towne from Topsfield, the clan that had given the Putnams so much trouble in the courts. The Putnams would have revenge against their enemies. Nurse's case, like those of Sarah Cloyse and Mary Esty, her sisters, cannot be separated from the vituperous politics of the Village clans.

On March 24, after Lawson had preached to the Salem Villagers and Ann Putnam Jr. had accused Nurse, she was brought to the Ingersoll tavern, held for a time, then transported up the steps to the meeting-house. She had traveled this route so many times, in other circumstances, that she must have felt the irony of her new role. Did it also frighten her? Not from the evidence of her replies to the magistrates' questions. At first they were gentle, for the magistrates presiding over the interrogations did not want to believe all they heard. Hathorne turned to the girls and asked if they recognized Nurse, which they did. She was the afflictor. Putnam and Williams cried out, and a bewildered but composed Nurse denied that she was the cause of their pain. "God will clear my innocency," she maintained. Hathorne for a moment might have wished it so, for he answered, "[T]here is never a one in the Assembly but desires it" more than he. Yet if she were guilty, he was convinced, "God [will] discover you." Hathorne here revealed that he believed in the medieval idea of ordeals, in which God demonstrated who was innocent and who was guilty. He needed a sign, and it came from Ann Putnam Sr., who rushed to the aid of her daughter by accusing Nurse. She said, "Did you not bring the Black man with you, did you not bid me tempt God, and dye." Goodwife Putnam verged on hysteria. She was not playacting, and her passion gave credibility to the girls' testimony. Her references to suicide must be taken seriously, for her daughter had exhibited the fits for almost two months, and the mother was beside herself with worry. Williams and Ann Putnam Jr. began wailing, and Mary Sibley and Elizabeth Hubbard, hitherto quiet, added their voices to the clamor.

Nurse was struck dumb by it all, and Hathorne, changing his tone, baited her. How could she have dry eyes when so much suffering poured out around her? What did Nurse say to the "grown persons" who joined the accusers? Hathorne again showed a little of his hand: he did not wholly buy the girls' accusations, but when their elders spoke—particularly Ann's mother—their words had to be weighed with care. Again, he offered Nurse an out: "Possibly you may apprehend you are no witch, but have you not been led aside by temptations that way[?]" "I have not," she replied. Again he hesitated, moved perhaps by Nurse's friends, who had begun lamenting as well. Hathorne now tried a different tack, one he would repeat in later hearings: Could the suspect help him explain the fits? "Do you think these suffer voluntarily or involuntarily?" he asked. Was it a trap? "I cannot tell," Nurse replied. He persisted, "That is strange[,] everyone can judge" (and had), but Nurse was at the end of her tether. "I cannot tell," she repeated. A good Puritan, she would not judge another. To have accused the girls of feigning was to charge them with perjury. To understand how the Devil worked was beyond her powers. Pressured, she finally guessed that the girls were not naturally afflicted but bewitched. Impressed by Nurse's calm, Hathorne gave her a last chance. Tituba loved Betty but affirmed that her specter, out of her control, must have afflicted the girl. Might not Nurse's apparition have done the same? Nurse was having none of it, however. Why do you "have me bely [belie] myself," she retorted, but she did allow that the Devil might take her shape.

Exhausted, sick, and overcome, Nurse had nevertheless produced the one argument that was irrefutable in defense. Osborn had already assayed it. No one could stop the Devil from assuming the shape of a good person and using His powers to hurt others. Even Increase Mather had conceded as much, and he was a believer in the malign powers of witches. Neither Nurse's defense nor her frailty deterred Hathorne from committing her to jail, no doubt to chain her there (for chains, everyone knew, prevented the witch's specter from escaping her body), but the argument would continue to trouble everyone in authority.

The girls were not done, however, not just yet. As she was taken away, no doubt fatigued, Nurse held her head to one side. Elizabeth Hubbard, closely observing the detainee, immediately bent her neck to the same side, and Abigail Williams cried out, "Set up Goody Nurse's head . . . the maid's [Hubbard's] neck will be broke." When Nurse's neck was forcibly straightened, Hubbard's head was magically restored to its normal posture.

A question comes to mind: If Nurse were a witch, and wanted to hide her crimes in darkness or secrecy as was the witches' custom, why did she harm the girls during the examination? By so doing, she not only proved that she was a witch but also violated the code of the witch: do nothing in public. Serious crimes required two attesting witnesses before the grand jury could indict. That is why the indictments against Sarah Bishop did not allege any of her older acts of witchcraft but only mentioned the harm she supposedly did the girls during her examination. The magistrates recognized this conundrum when they asked the suspects to explain what was wrong with the girls. Some of the accused replied that the girls were feigning. Others said the girls must be sick. A few conceded the possibility of witchcraft but denied their culpability. Some, like Nurse and later Elizabeth Proctor, directly addressed the girls and asked them to stop dissembling, to no avail. John Alden, an old sailor and ship captain, faced with a roomful of wailing girls supposedly struck down by his glance, asked the magistrates why they did not quake and quail before him if he had the evil eye. The question remains why anyone would assume that witches, who loved to act in secret, made a public display of their evil powers at a time when such a display would lead them to the gallows. The answer seems to be that the magistrates assumed the witches were so arrogant and so nasty that they did not care what anyone thought, or the witches believed that they could not be stopped. All of which, of course, made the magistrates more desperate to uncover and prosecute witches.

Parris might have doubted the testimony of a few servant girls and his own frail daughter, but he could not—for political reasons if for no other—ignore the sworn oath of Ann Putnam Sr. in his own meeting-house. A few days later, on March 27, with the second batch of suspected witches in custody, Parris went even further than had Lawson. Although the girls had extended their accusations to Nurse, whose status and reputation in the Village were impeccable, he refused to stem the tide or even divert it. There were demons, and he wanted to exorcize them. It would have taken a special kind of courage for him to try to stop the momentum of accusation, and he had never shown such courage. He no longer doubted that witchcraft had come to Salem Village and preached that "there are devils as well as saints in Christ's church," sinners and wicked people hiding in the covenant of the church. God knew how many these were and had given his true believers the means to discover the Devil's mischief. Beset himself, Parris cast his terrible anxieties among his congregants like seeds in planting time.

The effectiveness of Parris's preaching depended not on the scriptures to which they alluded but on the moral and emotional force of his discourse. Bent as he was by the cries of the afflicted, so his congregation was inclined. The book learning of Puritan ministers here merged into the crude way that ordinary people communicated with one another in the streets, just as the magistrates' formal proceedings were altered by the flood of oral testimony. People calling out in services, rumors flying all over, butting into the gliding specters of the witches in the rafters of the meetinghouse, made it nearly impossible for ministers to maintain church discipline. Whether Parris (or Lawson, for that matter) could have contained the contagion—bound down the Devil and His works—within the meetinghouse is a matter of conjecture. After the trials ended, Parris half apologized.

Nurse was confined to jail after her examination. It was a hard time for a woman her age. Sarah Osborn, a decade younger, died in jail that spring. Nurse was supported by her husband, children, and much of the community, but the accusers had time to prepare their case. On June 2 the magistrates sent out warrants to bring witnesses. Between then and June 29, they gave testimony. Thomas Putnam's family took the lead, protecting little Ann and pursuing their vendetta against Nurse née Towne. Like Bishop, Nurse was indicted for injuring the girls during the examination, but the grand jury heard more than that. The most telling testimony came not from the Houltons or the girls but from Ann Putnam Sr. To the grand jurors, her neighbors, she repeated her earlier testimony: on March 18, worn out from tending her child and her maid, she lay down to rest, but the specters of Cloyse and later Nurse had driven her to distraction. They demanded that she deny Christ and sign the Devil's book, but she resisted. And last but not least, on June 3, hearing her deposition of May 31 read one more time, she shrieked that Nurse had come back to pinch her.

It is entirely possible that Goodwife Putnam really did "see," that is, believed that she saw Nurse, and that with the vision came intense pain. Such hallucinations are routinely reported today. They are associated with severe emotional stress, and Putnam surely experienced that in these days. Indeed, she would not live many years after the trials. The stress was multiplied by the involvement of little Ann in the accusations. There is also evidence of personal animosity in Ann

Putnam Sr.'s testimony. She reminded anyone who might have forgotten (and no doubt informed her daughter) that Nurse's mother had been accused of witchcraft. Everyone assumed that mothers taught their daughters the magical arts. Others gave testimony against Nurse out of sheer bile, like Sarah Bibber, whom no one liked, and out of loyalty, like Nathaniel Ingersoll, who came to the aid of the Thomas Putnams on more than one occasion. But Ann Sr.'s compelling, trance-like evidence must have carried the prosecution's case.

On June 29 Nurse was brought to trial. The grand jury had indicted her, forced to choose between her still bewildered and increasingly enfeebled denials and the increasing strength of Ann Putnam's conviction that Nurse could visit harm through her specter. Nurse had herself, her friends, her husband, and her belief in God to defend her against the accusations. With these beside her, she fought back, even though it was an uneven battle. The best defense for a suspect was evidence of a good name. Testimonials of reputation and good character were admissible to make a case for the defense as well as to impeach the accusations of witnesses or victims. Contemporary English jurists like Matthew Hale instructed juries that they were to found their verdicts upon their own beliefs about personal qualities of defendants, informed but not dictated by what witnesses testified. As William Lambard wrote in *Eirenarcha*, his much respected and much copied manual for English justices of the peace, if the accused was a person of quality, jurors were to consider that in the defendant's favor; but they also were to take into account the defect of defendants' having evil parents, exhibiting a malicious nature, keeping bad company, having no job, or being accused of a similar crime in the past. One hundred years later, character remained a guide to New England juries.

Defense witnesses provided character references, but there was little these could do to refute spectral evidence, save to ridicule it or find it riddled with inconsistency. Some of the character testimony survives. The voices of friends and family spoke not to the legal issues but of duty and caring: Nurse was a person who had lived among the Villagers for many generations in good repute. How could they take her to be a witch now? At the behest of Goodman Francis Nurse, thirty-nine neighbors, including all of the Porters, as well as Benjamin and Sarah Putnam, and Joseph Putnam, testified that Goodwife Nurse was a woman of unblemished character. Nathaniel Putnam Sr. added his qualified agreement. The problem with character or reputation testimony in a witchcraft case was that, if the suspect were a witch, her misconduct would be so concealed that she might bear a good reputation in the daylight and carry on her mischief at night. Thus Rebecca Nurse could be a witch, despite her reputation.

If there were no learned counsel to plead for the defendants, there was a ready supply of popular legal wisdom, just as there was a folk supply of countermagic. A vernacular version of legal rights and duties was well established in the colony and governed ordinary affairs like the erection of fences and treatment of servants far more effectively than any book law. The essence of this customary lore was that the courts were not distant gladiatorial arenas but familiar and safe local institutions bringing together members of the same community to air differences and resolve disputes. Almost all of the defendants in the witchcraft trials had been in court for one reason or another before 1692, some sitting as jurors (although no women served in this capacity), others acting as witnesses, making complaints, or giving excuses for alleged misconduct. They were used to standing before local notables like Hathorne and Corwin. On such occasions, neighbors, codefendants, or coplaintiffs (in civil matters) shared experience with one another, creating a store of informal rules for getting along in the courthouse. Court clerks added their experience and good sense to the store of local legal cunning. For their part, the courts might order pains and punishments but generally returned the parties to their place in the community, even in cases of suspected witchcraft.

The defendants in the 1692 witchcraft cases were thus unprepared for the special court of oyer and terminer, whose function was not to make the community whole but to excise a few of its number to insulate the rest. The clerk, Stephen Sewall, was no help to the accused. Politely couched addresses to the bench did no good, in part because men like Stoughton and Richards were not from Salem. In vain, the accused relied upon the lore of law to save themselves. Nathaniel Cary sought a change of venue to protect his wife, Elizabeth, against the power of the girls. Sarah Buckley's husband, William, sought and obtained testimonials of his wife's Christian carriage from their ministers, John Higginson and Samuel Cheever. Confessing to everything, William Barker Sr. swore that "he has not known or heard of one innocent person taken up and put in prison," while his wife, accused with him, confessed but assured the judges that she was totally in the power of Goody Johnson and Goody Falkner, who threatened to tear her to pieces should she oppose them.

There are additional clues to defense tactics in the defendants' petitions to the court during and after the trials. In most cases the defendant made his or her mark at the end of the petition, meaning that it was dictated to another. One of these petitions is especially moving and reveals much about the conversation at trial. Its language is common, at times even coarse. Its sentiments mix the contrived and the resigned. Its force, however, is undeniable, even after three hundred years, and it proves that the condemned were not silent, passive, or acquiescent. Mary Esty was Rebecca Nurse's sister, a member of a Topsfield clan especially brutalized by the accusations and trials. To Phips and to the bench, she addressed her appeal:

That whereas your poor and humble Petition[er] being condemned to die Doe humbly begg of you to take it into your Judicious and pious considerations that your Poor and humble petitioner knowing her own Innocencye Blessd be the Lord for it and seeing plainly the wiles and subtility of my accusers by my Selfe can not but Judg charitably of others that are going the same way of my Selfe if the Lord stepps not mightily in. . . . The Lord above knows my Innocencye then and Likewise does now as att the great day will be known to men and Angells—I Petitione to your honours not for my own life for I know I must die and my appointed time is sett but the Lord he knowes it is that if it be possible no more innocent blood may be shed which undoubtedly cannot be Avoydd in the way and course you goe in. . . . I would humbly begg of you that your honors would be pleased to examine these afflicted persons strictly and keepe them apart some time and Likewise to try some of these confessing witchs[,] I being confident there is severall of them has belyed themselves and others as will appeare if not in this world I am sure in the world to come wither I am now going and I Question not but youle see an alteration of these things they say[.] My selfe and others having made a League with the Divel we cannot confesse I know and the Lord knowes as well shortly appeare they belye me and so I question not but they doe others[.] the Lord above who is the Searcher of all hearts knowes that as I shall answer it att the Tribunall seat that I know not the least theinge of witchcraft therefore I cannot I dare not belye my own soule.

Mary Esty respected the bench but was hardly in awe of it. Knowing that some of her neighbors had spoken untruths, she was partly confounded by the scope of their false witness and partly outraged by it. The accusers must have appeared to her to be in concert, an able perception, and the examining magistrates, rather than acting as sifters of evidence, seemed to be builders of the prosecution's case. In the process, they had not only given cues to prospective witnesses and bullied recalcitrant confessors but also allowed the accusers to listen to each other's stories and prepare a coherent final version. Esty urged the judges to give more weight to the inconsistencies in the accusers' stories, particularly when they were confessed witches themselves (the same point that Nurse made).

Esty's petition was more than a brief for the defense. She wanted the judges to know that she had not lost her faith—not in them and, more important, not in God. Her petition was a devotional, a confession not of guilt but of trust in the justice of the Lord. By testifying to her obedience, she made herself into one of the martyrs so much beloved by all sects in the seventeenth century. The Quakers had martyrs, as did the Puritans, the Roman Catholics, and the Anabaptists. Ironically, then, the trials had brought people like Esty and Nurse closer to the church and to God than they had been before. Witchcraft accusations restored or reinvigorated some defendants' godliness, surely the best proof of all that they were not witches.

Defendants could also challenge physical evidence produced at trial. Juries of midwives examined the suspects for unusual marks. Such examinations had a place in the lore of witchcraft and were used in English trials. In theory, the Devil's "familiar" needed a place at which to suckle. In the Salem cases, familiars were seen in both real and spectral form, but proof that one did not have such a teat did not alleviate suspicion. The result was a no-win situation for the defendant. Some, nevertheless, demanded a fair examination. For example, Rebecca Nurse asked for a different jury of midwives to examine her for "witchmarks," wanting only "most grand wise and skillfull" midwives for the task. She had already gone through two prior examinations with conflicting results.

The defendants and their witnesses not only attacked the reliability of physical evidence and the motives of the accusers but also impugned the motives of prosecution witnesses. One of Nurse's witnesses gave testimony that the identity of defendants was first suggested to the girls by their elders. John Tarbell testified that he was at the Putnam's house on March 28, and he then asked how Ann Putnam Jr. was able to identify Nurse. He nosed around and found out that Ann Jr. had not known who the "pale woman" was who afflicted her, and he discovered that the servant Mercy Lewis identified their neighbor as the culprit. "Thus they turned it upone one an other saying it was you and it was you that told her." Lewis's role as a leader of the gang was apparently already emerging.

The petition spoke silently, and other silences were as potent. For some of the older participants, particularly defendants like Sarah Good and Rebecca Nurse, silence could be tragic. They were hard of hearing and could not fully follow what was said, and so missed cues, misspoke themselves, and seemed, in the end, to be unresponsive to the questioning of the judges and the baiting of the accusers.

The accusers were sometimes silenced at trial, with the result that they could not coordinate their accusations as they had in the Village or outdoors. They developed instead a signing code (again the parallel to a modern gang suggests itself). They used facial expressions and touching—an ironic inversion of the "touching test" that proved a suspect was a witch—to communicate. "They did in the Assembly mutually cure each other, even with a touch of their hand, when strangled, and otherwise tortured," Deodat Lawson reported of the victims. This mime was intermixed with verbal commands to each other, as Lawson recalled: "They did also foretel when anothers fit was a-coming, and would say, 'Look to her, she will have a fit presently,' which fell out accordingly, as many can bear witness, that heard and saw it." The most impressive of all the silent moments involving the girls came, however, when the judges required that the defendants touch a girl to relieve her symptoms. This occurred periodically throughout the trials and made a strong impression upon the jurors. Increase Mather, joining Perkins and other authorities, objected to "ordeals" like placing a suspected witch in water to see if she would float, taking blood from the suspect, or burning her, but they did not rule out the touching test.

The fact remains that whatever Nurse might bring to bear in her own behalf, the judges directed the course of her trial. The jury found her not guilty, a verdict that might have reached far beyond her own case, for unlike those previously convicted, she was a woman of unblemished reputation and a church member in full communion. Her going forth "without delay" would have set a precedent that a good reputation could counter spectral evidence. The court intervened, in the person of Chief Judge Stoughton, according to the recollection of juryman Thomas Fisk, and directed the jury's attention to Nurse's words about Deliverance and Abigail Hobbs, two confessed witches who had turned informants. Nurse supposedly said, "'What, do these persons give in evidence against me now, they used to come among us.'" Stoughton told the jurors that such words could only mean Nurse admitted that she too was a witch. Some of the jurors asked the court's permission to retire to reconsider their verdict. When they retired, Fisk told his fellow jurors he was not certain what Nurse meant, and he wanted her to have the chance to interpret her remarks for the jury. The jury returned, and Nurse was asked what she meant, but old and hard of hearing, she missed the point. The jury then reversed itself and found her guilty. Informed too late of the change in her fortunes, she explained that she objected to being condemned by those who had admitted their miscarriages and weakness. Why should a jury believe such women and not her?

On July 19 Nurse, along with Elizabeth Howe (her sister-in-law), Sarah Wildes, Susannah Martin, and Sarah Good, were taken to gallows hill and hanged. The execution rituals of Puritan Massachusetts were fully developed (and similar to those in England). Everyone knew their roles, even the condemned. The public execution was the most severe of penalties. These were solemn occasions, in large measure because the role of public opinion was crucial to the effectiveness of the criminal justice system. There was no extensive police system—it was too expensive—and the general public had to keep order for itself. Neighbors watched and warned of crime. Posses of residents chased criminals. In Puritan Massachusetts, as in England, the accused rode to the gallows with a minister. The minister comforted the convict, showing the way in Christ's mercy for repentance, even in the shadow of the noose. The minister then read a sermon to the crowd, reminding them that they too would be judged. Ideally, the convict then confessed, discharging the guilt and allaying the fears of the multitude.

At her execution Sarah Good refused to confess, however, and warned the ministers who beset her that they would suffer for their misdeeds. Rebecca Nurse too declined to confess, and her demeanor was so decent and pure that many began to doubt the verdict. John Higginson, well along in years, attended as well, and was not pleased at what he saw in these sad events. Writing five years later, Higginson recalled that the events were tragic and left "in the minds of men a sad remembrance of that sorrowful time; and a doubt whether some innocent persons might not have suffered and some guilty persons escape." For, in truth, although the judges and juries acted "according to their best light," some of the rules the judges used were "insufficient and unsafe."

The refusal of the convicts to confess cast a pall over the entire ritual, for confession on the scaffold not only was good for the soul of the accused but also was necessary for the peace of the community. The guilty and the innocent were linked in their submission to the authority of God and the knowledge that all would have to be judged—those on the scaffold, and those below who watched. As historian Louis P. Masur has written, "The ritual of execution day required that condemned prisoners demonstrate publicly that they were penitent, and the execution sermons repeatedly pounded the chord of penitence." Confession in the moment before death could not be recanted and meant that the process itself was validated—that the truth had come out. The suspicion grew that Nurse had been wrongly convicted. If so, the rituals of punishment that cleansed crime, allowed the evildoer to repent, and made the community whole did not work.

But some were not deterred. Nicholas Noyes, Higginson's assistant in the Salem church, felt that the accused must be witches and deserved their fate. Along with Stoughton, he remained a dogged witch-hunter to the end. For the moment, Cotton Mather was jubilant, for as the number of cases increased, Andover defendants began to confess en masse to their supposed crimes. For Mather this was a proof that there had been a conspiracy, rather than a sign that innocent people so feared the animosity of the judges that they saw confession as their only chance to survive. At the beginning of August, Mather came out in the open with what he had kept to himself: his belief that the entire colony was beset with witches. "Our God is working of miracles," he wrote to another minister. "Five witches were lately executed, impudently demanding of God a miraculous vindication of their innocency. Immediately upon this, our God miraculously sent in five Andover witches, who made a most ample, surprising, amazing confession of all their villainies, and declared the five newly executed to have been of their company."

Throwing caution to the wind, on August 4, a day of fasting, he preached an apocalyptic sermon warning that the Last Judgment was near. The Devil must be worried, for He knew He would be judged as well. Although some scholars have found a shifting in Mather's position in favor of the admission of spectral evidence, perhaps due to the confessions at Andover, perhaps to the unsettled politics of the summer, the August sermon and the May letter to Richards are not much different. Mather merely emphasized in the former certain parts of the latter. In the sermon Mather confronted the armies of Satan and, like some Roman hero, stood at the bridge to bar their way into the city of God. With him stood a brave governor, Phips, a learned lieutenant governor, Stoughton, and eminent councillors. To John Foster, a member of Phips's council who did not sit in judgment of the witches, Mather reconfirmed his belief that the executions were warranted. Spectral evidence alone, he told Foster on August 17, should not prove guilt but should and indeed had led the court to a close examination of other evidence. The Devil could take the form of the innocent and even cure victims when touched by a falsely accused person, but Mather trusted the judges to see through the invisible wiles of the Evil One. Mather may have had in mind not the women but a far more dangerous group of convicts. There were scoffers and incendiaries in jail as well, men whose crimes included resistance to authority and criticism of the court. They included John Proctor, a tavern keeper, and the "little wizard," George Burroughs. These men and others waited in a Boston jail for their turn upon the gallows, two days hence.

CHAPTER 9

The Scoffers

John Proctor and George Burroughs were brought to trial on charges of witchcraft on August 2, 1692. Despite their spirited defense, they were condemned to die. The sentence was carried out on August 19, both men insisting to the end that the court was unfair to them.

The Puritans of eastern Massachusetts were no more authoritarian in their views or ways than any comparable group of English men and women. New England ministers and magistrates demanded the respect and obedience that any English pastor or justice of the peace could reasonably expect at home. But in the midst of the witchcraft crisis, challenges to authority took on more sinister shape. Critics of church and state cracked the wall of piety, allowing the sinuous Evil One to enter God's land. Indeed, cynicism and criticism were seen by some as evidence that a scoffer had already made a pact with the Devil. Tavern keeper John Proctor and minister George Burroughs were two of these scoffers, and they paid for their attitude with their lives.

The history of early Massachusetts was filled with remonstrances of religious and political dissenters. Some dissenters, like Roger Williams and Ann Hutchinson early in the century, were exiled for disputing the leading ministers' self-proclaimed monopoly on conscience. Others, like Samuel Gorton and Robert Child, were muzzled when they protested against the government. The Quakers were persecuted and driven from the colony. When a few of their number returned and persisted in their preaching, they were hanged. By 1692 the English Act of Toleration had forced Massachusetts authorities to allow Anglicans, Baptists, and Quakers'to live and worship in the towns, but toleration was limited and grudging. Proctor was associated with a small group of Quakers in Essex County, and Burroughs, though ordained a minister in conventional Puritan fashion, had veered toward the Baptist faith.

Otherwise, Proctor and Burroughs in their way were as typical of New England settlers as any of the Putnams or the Porters. Both in middle age, Proctor perhaps sixty, Burroughs in his early forties, they were not particularly successful, but they had families, reared children, did their jobs, and survived the rigors of life in a far-flung outpost of empire. Proctor was born in England and migrated to the New World, where he married first in 1660, then again in 1662; finally, after his second wife died in 1672, he wed Elizabeth Bassett in 1674. With Elizabeth he had five children. Burroughs was born in Virginia, went to Harvard, married first in 1673 and, after losing his first wife, married again. His second wife died, and her family, the Rucks, were among his detractors. They would even blame him for her death, perhaps reasonably, for he took her to the wilderness around Casco Bay, Maine, after he left Salem Village. In 1691 he married again, and he and his new wife had an infant daughter. The little girl had seven stepsiblings.

Both men had substantial stakes in their towns, but neither was a member of the establishment (or its equivalent in late-seventeenth-century New England). Proctor's tavern rivaled Ingersoll's in popularity. Burroughs made a decent living as a preacher. Personally, they were opinionated and unwilling to suffer foolishness. When the girls began to mention their names, they assumed that the girls would not persist in accusing men (which thus far was true), and moreover that strong men might put an end to the crisis by overawing the girls and their supporters. Unfortunately for them and their cause, they underestimated how powerful the girls had become or how many allies they had gained.

Proctor came under suspicion early in April, perhaps even earlier. A friend of his overheard one of the girls saying that they "must have sport," and that is why they turned their sights on the Proctors. By the end of the crisis, nine immediate family members, including the Proctors' three oldest children and Elizabeth's Bassett kin, had all been arrested. Most readers will know the family from Arthur Miller's moving dramatic recreation of their case in *The Crucible*. Miller read historical accounts but intentionally changed details. He made Proctor younger and more attractive than he was at the time of the trials and invented an adulterous relationship between Proctor and Abigail Williams, whose age he changed from eleven to seventeen years. In real life Proctor may or may not have had relationships out of wedlock, but they were not what he was accused of doing. Instead, it was the usual chorus of girls seeing Proctor's specter and feeling his pinching and punching.

The girls knew that he and his wife were vulnerable, for Proctor's wife and her kin were closely tied to Quakers. More important, perhaps, was the fact that the Proctors were almost certainly openly contemptuous of the proceedings. At Ingersoll's tavern, jest became a forerunner of real accusation. William Rayment, perhaps in drink (for there was a kind of tavern culture at Ingersoll's, as in most of the colonial watering holes, where common people could joke, toast, fight, gamble, and escape their betters' indignation), told Ingersoll's wife that he had heard Elizabeth Proctor would soon be examined. Not so, replied Goody Ingersoll, or she would have heard of it. Ingersoll was one of the semiofficial complaint makers, and he surely would have known and told his wife. But Rayment's companions were not so reticent— or so well informed. Some of the accusers were there as well and began to clamor, "there goody proctor, there goody proctor," and Goodwife Ingersoll had to silence them. The mockers then made jest of what had been, but moments before, the very sort of performance that was sending people to jail.

The first accusations fell not on Elizabeth Proctor alone, as some historians have written, but on both John and Elizabeth. He did not come to her examination unbidden and come under fire for his loyalty, as the common story reports, but had already been denounced by Abigail and Ann Putnam Jr. a week before the official inquiry into the couple convened. He and his wife were arrested and brought to a hearing in Salem, not the Village, on April 11. There Corwin and Hathorne were joined by Deputy Governor Thomas Danforth and councillor Samuel Sewall. Sewall had just returned from England and no doubt was curious to see what was going on in Salem. He had long been a judge on the Court of Assistants and probably had more than an inkling that Phips would ask him to sit on the court to hear Proctor's case.

Elizabeth Proctor's examination was not quite the same as those of her predecessors. Sarah Cloyse, who stood with her, was readily accused by all the girls, but for some reason they would not join against Elizabeth—perhaps they feared that they would be caught out by one of their number, Mary Warren, Proctor's servant. Asked outright if

{ *The Salem Witchcraft Trials* }

Proctor was her tormentor, Mary Walcott replied, "I never saw her so as to be hurt by her." Lewis, Putnam Jr., and Williams refused to speak—in effect, they hesitated to perjure themselves but kept their options open, for they acted as though some force had stopped their mouths. It was Indian John who first spoke against Elizabeth Proctor. Asked who was hurting him, he replied, "Goody Proctor." Unlike Tituba, his consort, he was in no danger. No one had accused him. Perhaps he just wanted to be a center of attention for once. In Salem he was an invisible man, rented out by Parris to cart refuse and clean tables at Ingersoll's tavern. He was enjoying himself. He was also helping Ingersoll, for the Proctor tavern took business away from Ingersoll's.

Elizabeth Proctor tried to defend herself: she knew nothing of Indian John's fits. But the logjam was broken, and Ann Putnam Jr. swore that Proctor was one of the witches. Then Abigail, moving to make sure that Mary Warren did not undermine this, or any other, accusation, reported that Elizabeth Proctor had told Abigail that Warren had written in the Devil's book and Abigail must as well. Not so, interjected Proctor, who reminded Abigail that "there is another judgment." Admonished by a mother figure, the two errant girls fell into a fit. There was Proctor on the beam, they shrieked. Some historians have argued that accusing women like Rebecca Nurse and Elizabeth Proctor was the only way the girls could vent their anger and frustration against their own mothers. Nurse and Proctor were substitutes. This is certainly possible and is well documented in modern clinical studies. Whether it happened in Salem must remain conjecture.

The girls did not confine themselves to mother surrogates. They discovered John Proctor perched on the crossbeam with his wife. The girls acted in concert, one warning that another was to be struck by the Proctors' specters, and the other girl immediately swooning. Benjamin Gould, a young man who had come as a spectator and became a witness, agreed that specters were flying about. But Proctor was the first man charged with witchcraft. What is more, unlike the women, Proctor was not likely to be reticent in his self-defense. He told Joseph Pope that if Samuel Parris would let him have Indian John, he would "soone drive the Divell out of him." In prison, he refused to bow to the authority of the judges. Instead, he wrote to the ministers of Boston that the judges and the accusers acted out of enmity and that he and his fellow defendants were condemned "already before our trials." He and the other inmates knew theirs was "innocent blood" and could prove that five of the confessed witches were lying, for they had been tortured. Turning Cotton Mather's anti–Roman Catholic sentiments back upon the minister, he wrote that the treatment of the prisoners was "very like Popish Cruelties." Proctor even asked the ministers to change the venue of the trials to Boston and to replace the bench with a fairer body. He got nowhere, but it was a measure of the man that he tried.

Sometime before the end of June, the grand jury refused to indict Proctor for attacking Mary Walcott, for she had denied it, but did indict him for a spectral assault on Mercy Lewis and Mary Warren, and thereby hangs a tale. Lewis was a cunning and convincing victim, but Warren's place in the story is the stuff of melodrama. When the Proctors were named witches by her girlfriends, Warren tried to refute their testimony. She had already begun to have fits, just like the other girls, and apparently Proctor had taken the rod to her to "cure" her of them. For a time the cure worked, perhaps because Proctor would not let Warren out of the house, but she soon found herself back in the company of Lewis and again became an accuser. She would not accuse the Proctors, however, and this put her outside the circle of girls, indeed it made her their target.

When Mary was brought before the magistrates a week after the Proctors were heard and arrested, she revealed that the girls had dissembled. She had turned informer on the accusers, and the gang reacted by denouncing her. The danger that Warren posed to the other young accusers went beyond breaking ranks. Bearing false witness, perjury in a felony case, was itself a felony, and lying in public was a misdemeanor. If Warren were believed, then the other girls had perjured themselves in a felony prosecution, and all their necks were exposed to the gallows. Did the girls know this? One assumes they knew that lying was a sin and that lying under oath was a crime.

Accused of witchcraft by her former friends, without aid—there were no parents or ministers or legal counsel to help her—she swooned. Coming to, she spoke wildly, then was taken outside for fresh air. She could not continue, but summoned privately before the two justices of the peace, she recognized that salvation in this world required confession and contrition, and she admitted that she had seen the Devil.

{ *The Salem Witchcraft Trials* }

With studied kindness, Hathorne and Corwin led Warren through her story. For two more days she provided the confirmation they needed against the Proctors and the conspiracy of witches. Later, like Hobbs, she would be brought periodically from jail to accuse some new suspect. Warren changed her tune just in time for everyone on the prosecution side to breathe easier, and no one more than the other girls. The magistrates did not warn Warren that her recantation could lead to her prosecution for lying or false witness. Instead, they were looking for evidence confirming their suspicion, turned now to certainty, that a conspiracy of witches threatened the colony.

Finally, there was a new accuser who came to the grand jury with a truly hideous tale. She was Elizabeth Booth, age eighteen, one of the outer circle of girls. On June 8 a parade of ghosts had supposedly appeared before her and accused the Proctors of serial murder. Robert Stone Sr. told her that the Proctors had killed him over a difference in "rekininge" (reckoning, or what he thought was due him). Hugh Jones materialized and reported that Elizabeth had killed him because he did not pay for a pot of cider. Elizabeth Shaw came and told Booth that the Proctors murdered her because she did not go to the doctor they recommended. The wife of John Fulton visited and accused Elizabeth of killing her because she would not give the tavern keeper's wife some apples. Finally, long-dead Doctor Zerubbabel Endecot came and accused Elizabeth of killing him in a quarrel about medical treatment. What the grand jury made of all this we cannot know, but these spectral crimes revealed to a deranged girl by the victims' ghosts demonstrate the hysteria that had gripped Salem.

On April 30 the girls reached out beyond the boundaries of eastern Massachusetts and tapped the shoulder of the "little wizard," George Burroughs. For many, drawn from all ranks of society, Burroughs was the archfiend, the leader of the witches. Confessed witches would later testify that he baptized converts to the Devil and led satanic masses in the dark woods. He was presently the minister in Wells, Maine, far away, but Maine's towns were governed by Massachusetts. Abandoning any pretense of judicial impartiality, William Stoughton bestirred himself to join in the attempt to bring down this coarse, muscular, self-confident, cunning little man.

The complaint was sworn to by Jonathan Walcott and Thomas Putnam. Hathorne and Corwin witnessed it and sent it to Elisha

Hutchinson, the magistrate in Portsmouth, New Hampshire. Evidently it bore the seal of the colony, for Hutchinson regarded it as an order from the governor and the council. Burroughs was apprehended and sent back to Salem in the custody of John Partridge (who styled himself the "feild marshall of the Provence of newhansher and maine"). By May 7 he was in Salem jail. By May 9 he had been removed to Boston, where he languished in jail, chained to prevent his specter from roving about. Other suspects were frightened to join him in his cell. They thought he was guilty, even if they knew their own innocence. Corwin and Hathorne were joined by Stoughton and Samuel Sewall to conduct the first examination of Burroughs. In early August evidence against him was collected anew, for the use of the grand jury. He was indicted and tried on August 12 and executed nine days later.

All of the girls—Mary Walcott, Mercy Lewis, Abigail Williams, Ann Putnam Jr., Elizabeth Hubbard, and Susannah Sheldon—accused him. Brought before him on May 9, they were a troupe of actors ready for this important engagement. He looked upon them, and they swooned as one. Betty was no longer there, but the other girls did not need her. Indeed, they did not need Burroughs, for he would not have been recognized by any of them but one—Lewis. When he turned to her, she fell into a dreadful fit. The magistrates were convinced by the girls and by the adults who repeated to the investigators Burroughs's own boastful words and his ill-usage of his wives. The indictments followed.

If each of the girls contributed one of the names, Mercy Lewis surely had singled out Burroughs. Lewis had lost her parents in an Indian raid on Falmouth, Maine, in 1689, and was taken into the household of Burroughs. Shortly thereafter, she came to live with Sergeant Thomas Putnam and his family, whose patriarch had led the fight not to pay Burroughs his back salary in a contested court battle and lost. Burroughs harbored no grudge, never dunning the town for the missing funds, but the Putnams evidently planned to add infamy to injury. In the time between his confinement and his indictment by the grand jury, others came forward, some from as far away as Maine, to confirm that Burroughs was the right-hand man of the Devil—in effect, the Devil's minister in Massachusetts.

On May 7, 1692, Lewis later told a grand jury, Burroughs's apparition had appeared and sorely tempted her. Unlike others, who testified to Burroughs's uncanny strength and conjuring tricks, and his supposed involvement in the deaths of his two previous wives, Lewis struck a personal note. Burroughs, she swore, had tried to trick her into signing the Devil's book, calling it a "fashion book." Had he tried to tempt her into sex with a gown, something her parents' death denied her? Deponents in this case and other cases described the book as the Devil's ledger, but not Lewis. He persisted, she demurred. "I have often been in his study but I never saw that book there," she told the magistrates. Two days later, she recalled, Burroughs "carried me up to an exceeding high mountain and shewed me all the kingdoms of the earth and tould me that he would give them all to me if I would writ in his book and if I would not he would thro me down and brake my neck."

The imagery is again compelling and distinct from the common charges. Other deponents testified that the Devil or the black man had promised them power or trinkets, or that another witch had carried them into the air, but never to the top of a mountain and never to ecstasy. The resemblance to Matt. 4:8 cannot be ignored. Lewis adapted the basic story line: the Devil carried Jesus to the mountaintop and offered Him the riches of the world should He but consent to pay homage to the Evil One. Begone, Satan, Jesus replied, and so did Mercy Lewis. But why did she borrow this imagery? Surely she had heard it at sermon time, but unlike other passages in Scripture, it resonated for her because it helped her organize her memories.

At first blush, one might regard this as a case of confabulation, in which memories of different events are incorrectly matched in a person's mind. Surely Burroughs had not carried her to the top of a mountain. Yet Burroughs, twice widowed, might have made some kind of sexual advance to fourteen-year-old Mercy, which she suddenly recalled. Or perhaps she had finally decided to admit aloud something that had troubled her for years. The language is allegorical, Mercy merging what she remembered with her own dark fears, but the structure of promise and threat is common and well documented in sexual abuse cases. The threat includes punishment for revealing advances as well as resisting them. Mercy recalled that she replied to Burroughs, "I would not writ if he had throwed me down on 100 pitchforks." Again the language is hers and reflects her fear of a man whose physical prowess amazed many. Lewis had a wonderfully vivid imagination and perhaps a growing attachment to Scripture, but the sexual connotation of "pitchforks" cannot be dismissed out of hand. In her equally compelling denunciation of George Jacobs Sr., another older man with a randy reputation, she recalled him beating her with sticks to make her sign his copy of the Devil's book.

But, as we have seen, the girls could not bring down a suspect by themselves. Here they had help. Burroughs was his own worst enemy. Since leaving Salem, he had not had an easy life. War had returned to Maine, and with it no one was safe. He had seen another round of raids and survived, a testimony to his toughness. He simply did not recognize the danger that the accusations posed to him. He scoffed. A small man, from each episode others recounted of his uncanny strength and prowess, he gained increased notoriety, which he seemed to court. There was something of the trickster in him, a willingness to fool, a delight in overcoming obstacles, not always in the most moral way. Perhaps this came of his living so close to the Indians, for whom the trickster was an admired (if not always trusted) character. Even in English culture, the cunning man, who knew more of lore than law, was a respected and feared figure.

For example, when Elizar Keyser came up to Burroughs's room in Thomas Beadle's house in Salem, four days before the May 9 hearing, Keyser was hesitant, for he was sure that Burroughs was the "chief" of the witches. Later, after Burroughs learned of Keyser's apprehensions from a friend, Captain Daniel King, Burroughs and Keyser happened to meet. Burroughs engaged in a little staring contest with the frightened Salem man. The stare did its work: not only was Keyser cowed, but later he hallucinated balls of light up his chimney, even though his wife, called to the scene, saw nothing.

Over the past decade, Burroughs had assayed similar mind games in Maine. He spread stories of his ability to lift a flintlock by putting a finger in its muzzle and to carry a full barrel of cider above his head. He played tricks on his second wife's relatives, like Thomas Ruck, whom he apparently despised. His boastful words now returned to haunt him. Before the grand jury, on August 2 and 3, Samuel Webber and others testified that Burroughs was rumored to have unnatural strength. Hannah Harris swore that Burroughs told his second wife (at least the wife told Hannah) that Burroughs could tell what she did even when he was not present. When his wife fell ill, neighbors and his wife's family widely spread rumors that Burroughs was at fault. The rumors reached the Village, as Francis Hutchinson testified. Abigail put it best: there had been a small black monster in Casco Bay, and now he was among them. Sarah Bibber, always ready to contribute, added that Burroughs's apparition went about at night in a black coat tormenting the girls (and Sarah Bibber).

Burroughs had other powerful enemies. The Putnams remembered him with venom and saw this as a chance for revenge. All but Joseph Putnam joined in the depositions against Burroughs. All the Putnams could do was testify that they believed the girls and saw the girls' agony. It was not probative evidence, for it rested upon the veracity of the girls, but as evidence that the family was behind the prosecution, their depositions could not be ignored. The two Anns said more. Little Ann claimed to be tortured by Burroughs's specter, and Ann Putnam Sr. told of his powers over his deceased wife. The ghost of the woman had come to her and related how Burroughs had murdered her. Rumor said that both of his wives had died under strange circumstances. The Rucks also pursued him, for with his new marriage his children by his second (Ruck) wife might be disinherited. Perhaps he even intimated that eventuality to irritate them.

Then there was the matter of his refusal to come to religious services or to baptize his younger children. When he was examined by the magistrates, on May 9, he explained that he was a full member of the church in Roxbury but could not recall when he last had communion, and he admitted that his younger children had not been baptized. Some scholars have argued that Burroughs had become a Baptist, refusing to accept the legitimate authority of his fellow Congregationalist brethren. Certainly, by acting as a Baptist, Burroughs lost whatever immunity he might have had as a minister against the claims of the girls. To the grand jury Abigail Hobbs and other confessors related that Burroughs was the antithesis of the good Puritan minister, for he administered the sacraments to the witches. He inverted the role of the clergy, just as evil women like Sarah Good and Bridget Bishop turned motherhood upside down by hurting children.

One question was not addressed by the court, or even by Burroughs's accusers. If Burroughs was a mischievous braggart and a cunning man facing a serious accusation of crime before what he must have expected would be a hostile crowd, why did he allow himself to be brought to trial? He could have run. Others had. Perhaps he thought himself guilty of some of the charges. He had been vain and boastful. He may have dabbled in the magical arts as well. Surely he had intimated as much to people, to impress and even frighten them. Coming back to Salem was a way of putting himself to the test, but it was not likely to be the same sort of moral self-examination as motivated the young women who confessed, for Burroughs returned contumely and venom to those who accused him. Perhaps he meant to face down his accusers. He had great confidence in his strength of mind as well as his physical prowess. Like the Proctors, he may had intended to put a stop to the entire proceedings, although by this time it was an act of great bravado. Everyone's heart was set against him.

Burroughs's trial is one of the few that Cotton Mather recounted from documents given him by Stephen Sewall and firsthand impressions related by the judges. Burroughs must have cut a distinctive figure. These were face-to-face events in a culture still dominated as much by sight and touch as by books and official documents. Observers recalled that, unlike most of the defendants, Burroughs challenged a number of his jurors. He carried on his defense vigorously and in the end directly addressed the jury. To his accusers, he seemed to be just what Abigail had called him, a little black monster. Indeed, witnesses equated him with the powerful little man in black who had caused them to fear for their souls. Of course, he was a small, strong, articulate man, which made fantasy blend into reality.

On August 19 Mather went to view the execution of the objects of his dire warnings and found that life did not exactly follow his art. George Burroughs, allowed to speak, said the Lord's Prayer perfectly, something folklore said was impossible for a witch to do, and greatly moved the crowd. Mather had to intercede, reminding people that Burroughs was duly convicted. But the minister was shaken, and more shocks were to come, for the confessors had begun to recant. The day before he was scheduled to die, Burroughs met with one of his accusers, Margaret Jacobs, at her request. She sought his pardon; he forgave her. In a letter to the honorable judges, dated August 20, the day after the executions, Margaret Jacobs admitted that "through the magistrates' threatenings, and my own vile and wretched heart" she had "confessed several things contrary to my conscience and knowledge, tho to the wounding of my own soul." Her confession had led to the execution of her grandfather (George Jacobs Sr.) and Burroughs. Her father was under indictment; her mother was crazy with worry; and Margaret was repentant. She recalled that at her examination she was frightened by the spectacle of the girls' antics and since that time had regretted the false confession that fear had drawn from her. She had implicated Burroughs "to save my life and have my liberty." Now she wanted the court to know that she was not a witch and never had been. Confessions had been Mather's surest sign of the Devil's work. The recantations made him pause.

While Mather waffled, his Boston counterpart Samuel Willard steadfastly admonished his congregants to check their credulity. Willard, like Mather, had seen children in agony of demonic possession but had acted differently, and by so doing had prevented a witchcraft crisis. In 1671 Willard, then a young minister in Groton, Massachusetts, kept a record of the unaccountable behavior of Elizabeth Knapp, a seventeen-year-old serving girl in his household. In the fall of the year, she had apparently been possessed by spirits, and her possession attracted colonywide attention. As Willard told the story, on October 30 Elizabeth began to act out in violent fashion. She shrieked, leaped about, and tried to harm herself. There would be moments of calm, followed by more fits. The seizures went on for three months, over the course of which Elizabeth would confess her sinfulness repeatedly in piteous terms. Her behavior attracted attention, and Willard sought help. Doctors admitted that they were stumped, but as she began performing for larger audiences, she began to intimate that she was bewitched. In the last phase of her seizures, she twice tried to name her assailant, but Willard would not let her accuse anyone. Willard kept a detailed record of the events, which he sent to Increase Mather, who then included it in his *Illustrious Providences*.

Knapp went on to marriage, a houseful of children, and a normal life. Willard, who came from one of the best families of the colony—indeed, was one of its leading native sons—went on to the pastorship of the Third Church of Boston and there preached a more optimistic version of Calvinism than Cotton Mather would tolerate. Ministering to his congregation in that terrible summer of 1692, Willard must have recognized the difference between his technique and Mather's. He had urged Knapp not to blame others; Mather, in the Goodwin case of 1688, sought the names of witches. More important, the different outcomes of the cases troubled Willard. Throughout the late spring and summer of 1692, he restated Perkins's cautions against hasty judgment in strong and pointed terms. In June he warned against defamation of neighbors, urging love and forgiveness instead. He told his parishioners, one of whom, Edward Bromfield, kept careful notes, that the Devil could fool anyone (by implication, even the magistrates), although Willard was careful not to impugn the wisdom of the judges directly. The rush to judgment in the Salem trials ignored these basic truths, replacing them with imaginary specters. Judges Peter Sergeant and Samuel Sewall were members in good standing of his church, but so was John Alden, who fled jail. Willard's warnings, for the time being, went unheard.

More than the pious farewells of the women hanged, the rumblings of the scoffers had given pause to the ministers, but the trials went on, and with their final sessions came the episode that has come to epitomize the atavism of the whole crisis. Giles Corey, the hardest of the hard men, refused to accept the authority of the court itself. He pled not guilty but would not take part in the trial; the judges turned to an older English method to force his compliance: covering him with heavy stones until he changed his mind. *Peine et fort dure,* pressing a person to make him answer the charges against him, had never been used in Massachusetts. What would come of Corey's stubborn courage when it was bound down by the fanatic persistence of the court?

CHAPTER 10

The Hard Man

New England was settled only sixty years before the witchcraft trials, and a man or woman of seventy might well remember the hardships of those first days. Indeed, in 1692 one had only to travel twenty miles to the north or west to learn that life was still brutish, nasty, and short. Such men and women had to be hardened to the blows of fortune and inured to the cruelties of war, starvation, and abandonment. In 1692 Giles Corey was nearly eighty years old. He had seen it all and then some, and he would not yield to a court that told him he was a wizard. In his refusal to "put himself on king and country," the term for standing trial in those days, he became a final martyr to the witchcraft mania. On September 19, three days before his wife, Martha, Sarah Esty, and six other convicts were hanged, he was pressed to death with heavy stones. A hard man, he died in the hardest way of all of them.

We cannot determine what motivated him. He must have spoken in his refusal to take part in the trials, but what remains from the anecdotes that others told is a stubborn old man who knew that he would be condemned and refused to admit to the legitimacy of the proceedings. He was born in 1612 in England, and came to New England sometime before the 1660s. With his first wife, Margaret, he had four daughters. She died, and in 1664 he married Mary Britt, who passed away in 1684. His detractors would later say that the ghost of his second wife had come to them and accused him of murder. An old man, he took another wife a year later, Martha Rich. She was twenty-five years younger than he, pious where he scoffed, and picky where he was ornery. Martha also had had a previous marriage, ending in the death of her husband. Together Giles and Martha made a life in the southwestern corner of the village as prosperous farmers, full members of the church, and, like Nurse, repositories of folk wisdom.

So when the news reached them in early March of the girls' accusations, they were skeptical, and when they had been named witches by the girls, they became downright angry. Such nonsense had to be stopped. Martha had a reputation for scolding neighbors in public and using strong language. Perhaps her forwardness made her a suspect. Deciding to put the girls in their place, Martha challenged the investigation. Martha confronted Sheriff Edward Putnam on March 12 and denied the charges. Hearing through gossip that she was denounced, Martha told the sheriff that she had anticipated his arrival. He reported this to Hathorne, who took it as an evidence that Martha was a witch. Two days later, she visited little Ann, for older women were expected to visit the sick, but Ann was already capable of fine dissimulation, and she had the other girls to help her. Martha then planned to trap her accusers by proving that they did not know what she wore as a specter, but Putnam and the magistrates merely took her efforts as evidence that she had a guilty conscience.

At her formal examination, on March 21, "a child" murmured to Cheever (and he dutifully recorded), "There is a man whispering in her ear." Alert to the presence of the Evil One, Hathorne increased the tempo of his questions, badgering the old woman. She denied all, but her denials became rote, no longer compelling Hathorne to take them or her seriously. He offered her "the out"—a technique used by police to this day: "Why, confess," he suggested, and she would feel much better. She refused, maintaining her innocence. Then Abigail cried out, and as one the girls became distracted. Mercy Lewis saw Martha Corey's specter swing an iron rod (a spectral one, presumably), and two of the other girls dodged it. When Corey laughed at their antics, they redoubled their efforts. Corey bit her lip; the girls produced bloody lips. She had an arthritis attack, clenching her hands, and they writhed, their hands twisted in a cruel but effective mockery of her pain. She was committed to Salem jail. Parris wrote the verbatim account. Cheever was busy with the girls.

At first Giles was confused. Was his wife a witch? They had not been married long, and he was as bewildered as anyone at the antics of the girls. He seemed to waver, at least according to some of his neighbors' accounts. Then his resolve hardened. He must have let everyone know that he would have no more of this. The girls once again acted quickly. Within two weeks they complained to Cheever and to

John Putnam Jr. that they had been attacked by Giles Corey. Cheever and Putnam swore out a complaint, and the magistrates ordered Giles to appear along with the girls and a number of other witnesses. On April 18 Corey was examined, and again the girls writhed on cue. No one remarked, for the record at least, on the convenience of it all, or why Giles would reveal himself a witch when he was already under close suspicion.

The old couple languished in jail for nearly five months before coming to trial, hardly the speedy trial promised in the old charter. As they were shuttled from Ipswich to Boston, to Salem, and back to Boston, their health and strength began to fail. Giles Corey, who already could see the handwriting on the death warrants, deeded his hundred-acre farm to his two sons-in-law. English law took from convicted witches their personal goods (called *chattels*) but not their land. Burroughs's third wife had already sold his goods, but like Proctor and a number of others, the jailed Corey's personal effects were seized by Sheriff George Corwin and sold.

Whether this "confiscation" was legal under Massachusetts law is still a matter of dispute. The *Lawes and Liberties* had explicitly ended the English practice of taking away the property of convicts from their families, but the old laws had been suspended. The new laws were to be "in conformity" to those of England, which might have imported the English rule of "escheat" of felons' wealth to the Crown; but when the colonial legislature met again in October 1692, under the new charter, the lawgivers reinstituted the old bar on forfeiture and confiscation. Plainly, the members of the colonial assembly did not want the English law on this issue to come to America, but that was three weeks after the Coreys were gone to their reward.

Giles and Martha Corey had to wait for trial because jails all along the coast were filled with suspected witches. By early September the jails were overflowing with nearly two hundred persons accused and awaiting disposition of their cases. Colonial jails were flimsy holding pens where suspects waited for trial or bail. Sometimes the wood was so rotten that those incarcerated could knock down the walls and walk away. In 1680

Josiah Gatchell testified that he knew Salem prison was not sufficient, for any man having no instrument except his own hands could come out as he pleased. . . . He saw one man pull up one of the boards overhead in the prison with his hand, going into the chamber of the prison, and others went out under the groundsill and some went out next to the watchhouse. . . . They found not one room there that was sufficient to keep in a man who had the dexterity of an ordinary man.

And Gatchell would know, having spent much of the late 1670s and early 1680s in the Salem jail on a variety of charges. Most of the inmates were debtors who either had refused to pay what they owed or had not yet signed a statement indicating that they had no resources to pay the debt. All prisoners paid for firewood and food or had it delivered by friends and family. The poor in prison thus suffered most. Jailers—called *keepers*—were jobbers and often negligent. They allowed suspects to go home and to receive visitors freely.

The prisoners talked to each other in their cells or in the yard. Most stayed, expecting justice, too tired to risk flight, or simply resigned to their fates. Osborn, shuffled back and forth between Boston and Salem, died, as did Roger Toothaker, Lydia Dustin, and Ann Foster. The suffering inmates spoke to the court through their families, whose courageous and persistent petitions raised the spirits of the defendants. These addresses were respectful, the petitioners couching their appeals in the language of good subjects of a lawful sovereign. The petitioners begged the court to allow their aged relatives to go free on bond pending their trials or, failing that, to order improvement in the suspects' living conditions. The court did nothing.

Some prisoners, particularly in Boston, were allowed to roam more freely and used that freedom to arrange with friends to escape. Mary and Philip English broke jail, leaving behind their spacious house, its furnishings, its silver plate, and the mixed feelings of their neighbors. Sheriff George Corwin swiftly seized their china and linens, for fleeing suspects' goods were forfeit. Unfortunately, he acted before they were indicted, making his confiscation illegal. Daniel Andrew, scarcely less wealthy than English and more closely allied to the Porter clan, had more friends and still fled. Edward and Sarah Bishop left, proving that ordinary folks could flee as well. With them went John Bradstreet, a justice of the peace in Andover whose refusal to sign any more arrest warrants brought suspicion upon him; Elizabeth Cary, who flew with the help of her husband, Nathaniel; George Jacobs Jr., the most feared of all the incarcerated, to hear the girls tell it; and Hezekiah Usher and John Alden, undoubtedly with the help of friends. They all risked forfeiture of their property, which was considerable, but life was more precious.

Giles Corey was to be tried on September 19. The grand jury heard evidence against him sometime between September 9 and 17 and indicted him. Some of the testimony presented to them is preserved. Ann Putnam Jr. swore that she saw the specter of Corey on April 13, and that he wanted her to write in his (that is, the Devil's) book. Of course she refused. He tormented her during the April 19 hearing and periodically thereafter, leaving his jail cell in spectral form. Evidently his chains did not keep him in his cell. In her opinion (now expert) he was a "dreadful wizard." Unremarkably, Mercy Lewis reported the same misconduct from him in virtually the same words and agreed that he was a "dreadful wizard." Mary Warren and Sarah Bibber, in somewhat less fulsome terms, recounted Corey's assaults on them.

Elizabeth Woodwell and Mary Walcott testified that they saw Giles Corey in his accustomed place in the meetinghouse after he was incarcerated. Evidently his spirit still enjoyed the solace of a sermon. Why a witch should want to come back to church and sit patiently through the service was not disclosed. Benjamin Gould reported that Giles and Martha had visited him when he lay abed and that afterward he had a stitch in his side. Later, seeing Giles and John Proctor together, he felt a terrible pain in his toes. Susannah Sheldon told the grand jurors that she had met a ghost who told her that Giles Corey had murdered his first wife, and only the fact that his last wife, Martha, was a witch saved her from her predecessor's fate. John DeRich, a teenager whose mother was under investigation, added that Giles Corey's specter had come to his house and demanded platters that he might feast—this on September 5, with the trial but two weeks away. Hannah Small and Martha Adams agreed that when they came by DeRich's house, the flatware was gone. Finally, Elizabeth and Alice Booth stated under oath that they saw over fifty witches gathered the night of September 12 and that Corey appeared to serve bread and wine for the witches' sacrament. He offered it to the Booths, but they refused. There was no mention of the DeRich flatware in their testimony.

A last blow fell before the trial. On September 11 Pastor Noyes led the Village congregation in an excommunication of Martha Corey. A week later, the members of the church purged Giles Corey from their midst. The Coreys died outside of the comfort of the church. This was not so damning for a Puritan as it would be for a member of a more liturgical faith. The church did not save, nor was it the Body of Christ. God alone saved, and He alone knew whether the Coreys were among the elect. Still, the slap must have stung. The excommunication could not have been unanimous. The Coreys identified with the pro-Porter faction of the Village church, and men like Francis Nurse would never have assented to the old couple's disgrace. Eleven years later, a chastened congregation led by a new minster reversed itself and posthumously restored the Coreys to the privileges of membership.

The record contains one last fragment of evidence, a letter from Thomas Putnam to Judge Sewall given by the judge to Cotton Mather, probably on September 22, and published by Mather in his *Wonders of the Invisible World*. In it Putnam recounted Ann Jr.'s meeting with yet another ghost, a man wrapped in winding sheets who revealed to her that Corey had murdered him. It was amazing, Thomas Putnam concluded, for Ann did not know that seventeen years before an inquest had been held into the sudden death of a man boarding with Giles Corey. The man had died under suspicious circumstances, and Corey seemed the likely culprit. Yet, "as if . . . some enchantment had hindered the prosecution of the matter," Corey got off. But now he was to pay.

A nineteenth-century account suggested that Corey remained mute because he wished to protect his estate from being taken by the state. That may have been his understanding of the law, but in fact he did plead not guilty to the indictment and then refused to participate in the trial. By literally refusing to say his lines, he forced the judges to reach into their power to hold him in contempt, but pressing him to death exceeded those powers. Appeals to him to change his mind, by the court and by friends, were to no avail. Out-of-date English law required the court to ask the suspect three times to change his mind, but there is no evidence of how many times the Salem court approached Corey. Samuel Sewall reported that the gruesome public event took two days.

Corey brought the community back into the trials in a way that the women and men hanged on gallows hill did not. True, among those who watched Nurse and others like her on the gallows, there was a nagging feeling that the wrong people were being punished. When Burroughs died with the Lord's Prayer upon his lips, Cotton Mather had to quell the unrest of the crowd, but Burroughs did not take two days to succumb. In addition, Corey's death was unique; no one in the colony had seen such an execution—for that is what it became. Finally, by allowing himself to be crushed, Corey gave back fortitude and courage rather than spite and bewilderment, unlike Bishop, Good, and others.

By dying under the stones, Corey was testifying to his good name. He became part of the legend of the tragedy of Salem, perhaps more than any of his fellow defendants. William Wadsworth Longfellow gave Corey the immortal dying lines:

> I will not plead
> If I deny, I am condemned already,
> In courts where ghosts appear as witnesses
> And swear men's lives away. If I confess,
> Then I confess a lie, to buy a life,
> Which is not life, but only death in life.

Corey, the seventeenth-century New England hard man, in death became Corey the nineteenth-century romantic hero.

Meanwhile the judges had begun to sense that they might soon become targets of reproach not from witches but from the ordinary people. After the September 22 hangings they gathered at Stephen Sewall's house and planned what today would be called "spin control." To Cotton Mather, their minister, they gave the records of all the trials, so that he might write a book extolling the judges and defending the trials—his *Wonders of the Invisible World.* Then he or Sewall conveniently lost the actual trial records. There would be more trials, over fifty of them, but no more spectral evidence, only three convictions, and, by May 1693, pardons for all.

CHAPTER II

The End of the Trials

The brakes were applied to the careening trial court not by the outrage of kinfolk of the accused but by a segment of the educated elite of the colony. The two cultures—popular and learned—always so near each other in Puritan Massachusetts, had overlapped in the witchcraft crisis to a greater extent than ever before. The recollections of the panicky many had for a time displaced the learning of the educated few. Recognizing that this world turned upside down threatened the purity of the word they understood, and brought with it the specter not of witches but of social chaos, the ministers joined together to pull their congregations back from the brink of the abyss. But the ministers did not speak as one, or quickly, against the danger.

While Cotton was battling the Devil at arm's length, hurling sermons against the squadrons of specters that circled Salem, the Ministerial Association was in more or less continuous session. Unlike Cotton, numbers of them had traveled to Salem to see the first trials as well as the executions. They must have spoken among themselves on the trip and between times. Their advice against the use of spectral evidence had been misunderstood or ignored. Either way, they were not heard, and that rankled. To a man, they believed that the Devil was abroad, but His works—entire communities roiling in conflict; congregations slashing themselves apart; good men and women languishing in dungeons—were not the acts of witches.

Willard, frustrated by his fellow ministers' inaction, was already speaking against the trials, though not against the judges. Visiting his own parishioners in jail, he may even have helped some of them to flee. He wrote all his objections to the trials, beginning with his suspicions of the girls' veracity and ending with his thoughts on the power of the Devil to wreck a commonwealth, but was banned by the governor's proclamation from airing them in Boston. Secretly, he arranged for them to be printed, but with the misdescription that they had in fact come from the Philadelphia press of William Bradford.

Following English writers who objected to witch-hunts there, Willard insisted in *Some Miscellany Observations* that satisfactory proof of witch-craft was almost impossible to obtain. Cast in the style of a philosophical dialogue much like the first Puritan work on witchcraft, Henry Holland's *Treatise Against Witchcraft* (1590), Willard's message was simple: conviction by mere suspicion was "contrary to the mind of God . . . besides, reason tells us, that the more horrid the crime is, the more cautious we ought to be in making any guilty of it." But had not divines and lawyers given great weight to such presumptions? No, said Willard, Perkins and others had warned against conviction upon presumption—a clear slap at Cotton Mather's reading of earlier Puritan authorities. Instead, the judges must have a matter of fact "evidently done and clearly proved," that is, they must have proof of causation. This was precisely what the judges did not have unless they admitted spectral evidence. It was the specter that caused the pain, and only the victims could see, or professed to see, the specters. Yet even if the judges credited the girls' testimony, such specters could be created only by the Devil, and crediting spectral evidence thus made the Devil a creditable witness for the prosecution.

For his own part, Willard simply refused to believe the accusers. If their evidence could not be confirmed, "there will be no security for innocence." Indeed, one of the girls, Abigail Williams, had even accused Willard of being a witch, but, ushered out of the courtroom, she was told that she was mistaken. She took the hint and recanted. Willard insisted that history proved that innocent people could be sent to their deaths by such means, for they made the Devil an informer against Himself—surely the very sort of disordering of the world that the Devil enjoyed best. Willard knew that in the human heart there was room for "concupiscence," an impulse to serve an evil master, and for grace, the ability to rise above temptation.

Aware that Willard was busy with his own condemnation of the trials, seven of his brethren met in College Hall at Harvard, in Cambridge, on August 1 and asked Increase Mather for another statement on evidence. He was the acknowledged leader of the Ministerial Association, and the judges and the governor would have to listen to him. Had he not helped Phips become governor and brought the colony its new charter? He had stayed on the sidelines thus far, in part because he had gone on record in his *Essay* as favoring many of the assumptions the judges made, and in part because he strongly supported the current administration. Increase was a masterful politician. He waited until the trials were suspended at the end of the summer and then presented his work, *Cases of Conscience,* to the association on October 3. Willard was delighted, said so in a long preface, and, with thirteen of the other ministers, signed. Cotton did not, because he saw clearly that he and his father profoundly disagreed. Silently, he rushed ahead with a compilation of his summer sermons, accounts of the trials, and extracts from the books in his library that he used in preparing his letter to Judge Richards.

A copy of *Cases* was given to Phips, who read and understood its implications immediately. Unlike his son, Increase was a fine and forceful writer. Cotton Mather later judged that his father's tract was the reason Phips ordered the court to disregard spectral evidence. Phips also disbanded the court of oyer and terminer, then in recess, and temporarily reprieved the five who were in jail awaiting execution. The extent of Increase Mather's influence on Phips may be debated, but there can be no doubt that Increase had written what amounts to the first American tract on evidence in powerful and thoughtful prose. It is simply one of the great works of American legal literature.

Cases began with an address to the Christian reader that echoed Willard's injunction: the more execrable the crime, the more caution the accusations required. There was a Devil, and He reveled in the admiration of His witches, but Christian charity and legal wisdom demanded close attention to the rules of evidence in cases of witchcraft. Increase then offered two progressively demanding tests of evidence. First, he insisted, "Charity is not to be foregone as long as it has the most [evidence] preponderating on its side," a theological version of the "probable-cause" test the modern grand jury actually uses. Applying it to those suspected of witchcraft in Salem might have resulted in fewer indictments. Grand juries had not been particularly charitable in these cases, although they had found "no bills" on some occasions. Increase then turned to the standards for proof at trial. If the testimony and other evidence "do not infallibly prove the crime against the person accused, [the court] ought not to determine him guilty of it." This requirement exceeded Perkins's and other English ministers' cautions and presaged the modern doctrine of "beyond a reasonable doubt." Reasonable doubt is what would stay a prudent person when confronted with the evidence.

Increase continued that reliance upon spectral evidence or the ordeal of forcing the suspect to touch a victim "would subvert this government, and disband, yea ruine, Humane Society." In support of his admonition, he warned that devils could impersonate innocent people, even those who were truly godly, and delighted in the commotion and mistrust such impersonations caused—precisely the defense Osborn and Nurse raised and Hathorne dismissed at the pretrial hearings. Bewitched persons might think that anyone touching them was the witch, and so would be cured, for many supposed witchcrafts were natural distempers, and the power of the imagination was strong enough to restore these people to health, as it had rendered them ill in the first place. Indeed, if only God could heal such ailments, then no witch's touch could cure a sick person. To think otherwise was blasphemous. Finally, just as in the crediting of spectral evidence, using the ordeal of touching to determine guilt was indulging in the Devil's own work. Why should the sudden recovery of the victim be more believable than the protestations of innocence of the defendant?

Increase concluded that evidence of witchcraft must be as clear as evidence of any other felony. This was Willard's point, and Increase elaborated on it. A free and voluntary confession was good proof, if the confessor had full possession of her faculties and was not coerced, but confessions that included impossible things suggested coercion or derangement. For this reason, the confession of one witch against another was not to be accepted on its face. The malice that one suspect might bear another could easily motivate such accusations. So, too, the testimony of two honest persons to the fact of witchcraft— seeing and hearing the suspect do her mischief—had to be credited, but none of these had appeared in the Salem trials, save those testimonies rooted in spectral evidence. In the end, "It were better that ten suspected Witches should escape than one innocent person should be condemned."

While the Mathers struggled among themselves and with their critics to make the story come out right, Phips tried his hand at damage control. His imperial masters had to be informed, and Phips had to protect his position. In October he reported to the English authorities that on his arrival the province had been aboil with accusations. To sift through the claims he had appointed a special court, then left to defend the colony's northern frontier. When he returned he had found dissatisfaction brewing not only with the conduct of the trials but with his administration as well. Most vexing, "I found the Devil had taken upon him the name and shape of severall persons who were doubtless innocent and to my certain knowledge of good reputation for which cause I have now forbidden the committing [to jail] of any more that shall be accused without unavoydable necessity, and those that have been committed I would shelter from any Proceedings against them wherein there may be the least suspicion of any wrong to be done unto the Innocent." Phips asked for instructions, and in the meantime had forbidden anyone to write or publish comments on the affair (a ban which Willard had already violated). He had heard the groaning of the innocent, but the politics of the affair were even more trying to him. Too many important people had come under assault, giving a lever to the popular party—the party opposed to Phips.

Others had already stepped into the fray with their own lately be-gotten misgivings. Thomas Brattle, whose professed respect for author-ity was so strong, he said, that he would "sooner bite my fingers' ends than willingly cast dirt on authority, or any way offer reproach to it," nevertheless on October 8 wrote a letter to a friend for private circu-lation. Brattle asserted, "I never thought judges infallible; but reckoned that they, as well as private men, might err." When such errors were "fundamental" and perverted justice, they undermined genuine author-ity and had to be exposed. Because a "poor child" had a fit and accused men and women of proven repudiation, judges who had known the suspects for years and thought them honorable and pious now sen-tenced them to death. Brattle, a man of science, condemned the cre-dulity of the judges, believing as they did that the touch of a suspected witch might cure a possessed girl of her affliction.

This "Salem philosophy" was false, and even if it had some basis in the supernatural, it could easily be manipulated by the Devil Him-self. The admission of "spectre evidence" made the accused guilty without the power to prove their innocence. Brattle's sarcasm gave way to admiration when he thought of those who had, covertly and overtly, resisted the witch-hunt. Boston justices of the peace had allowed men and women accused of witchcraft to leave the province, sometimes by breaking jail, and did not pursue them to their sanctuaries. Men of parts like former governor Simon Bradstreet, Danforth, Increase Mather, and Willard spoke out against the conduct of the trials. Even in Salem, there were many who quietly opposed the whole affair.

In the Village an uneasy truce prevailed. Tentative efforts to repair the damage to families were pathetic. For example, when the Essex County Quarterly Court met on September 27, 1692, the selectmen and grand jurors of Ipswich reminded the judges that they must provide for the care of Samuel Willard's fatherless children, some of whom were quite young. Corwin and Hathorne ordered that they be placed "into good and honest families." The agony of the Village and its neighbors made little lasting impression upon the local courts. The families of the accused did not sue the accusers for false witness or defamation. In the quarter sessions civil courts, Corwin and Hathorne presided over business as usual. The Putnams and their allies continued to dominate the lists of trial and grand jurors in the quarterly courts and later, in 1694, in the new courts of common pleas and general sessions of the peace.

Early in 1693, when the trials were winding to their close and the detainees were returning home, the Villagers attempted a reconciliation of sorts, but the effort was short-lived for the same reason that the original crisis had erupted. People could not talk to each other without becoming embroiled in old animosities; conversation became argument, and argument exploded into accusation. Parris himself tried to preach conciliation, but his words failed to soothe, for he remained convinced that some of the more stiff-necked congregants still mocked him and the church by refusing to come to the Lord's Supper. He disclaimed any blame for what might have been miscarriages of justice. Parris's supporters could pay his salary, but for the next year and a half they could not gain control of the Village meeting or of the committee it elected. The meetinghouse needed repairs, but none were made.

Petitions flew back and forth between the Village and the General Court. The dissenting Villagers, as Parris dismissively called them, were led by the Nurse and Cloyse families. They had suffered much in the witch-hunt but, underwritten by the Porters, continued their struggle for control of the pulpit. The issue had become clear: Parris had to assume some responsibility for his too-ready belief in the guilt of his own neighbors and for his lack of charity toward those who opposed him. Under far lighter criticism, his predecessors had resigned, but Parris hung on, grimly resisting attempts to call a convocation of ministers to hear the dissenters' grievances, labeling the protests "libels" in the church record (which he kept), and managing to prevent the meeting for over a year after the General Court had ordered it be held.

The General Court, to which the Villagers had turned so many times in the past, sat only once during the trials and quickly adjourned. It met again in the second week of October 1692, and the families of the incarcerated immediately approached it. Their petitions were couched in humble, even piteous, terms, for they trusted the newly reconstituted assembly to aid them. Before the charter was revoked, the General Court had been just that—the deputies (the lower house) and the magistrates or "assistants" (the upper house) heard both civil and criminal law cases. Under the new charter, it was merely the legislature, but it could still create courts, as well as grant relief through private bills and acts.

John Osgood and eight others approached this "honored Court" in October. Osgood's wife and their loved ones remained in jail, no threat to anyone, without proper food, clothing, or heat as the winter approached. Might they not be sent home "under bond"? A flood of petitions followed theirs. At first their aim was to ease the suffering of those in jail. No one attacked the jurisdiction of the court of oyer and terminer, the motives of the judges, or the outcomes of the previous cases, although out of doors the criticism had grown loud. Aided by family, numbers of the prisoners themselves petitioned for redress of grievances. From Ipswich jail, the widow Penny and nine others asked that they might return home on bail for the winter, "for we are not in this unwilling nor afrayed to abide the tryall before any Judicature apoynted in convenient season," but winter in the jail would surely kill some of the older prisoners and perhaps one of the prisoners who was pregnant and another who was nursing a ten-week-old baby. Francis Dane, pastor in Andover, wrote to the assembly. He had lived in the town for "above" forty years and knew the Carriers, the Johnsons, and the Barkers, entire families of his church that languished in jail on the basis of confessions extorted through "flatteries" and "threats." He had heard and seen no evidence of witchcraft from any of them, particularly from his daughter, Elizabeth Johnson, or his granddaughter, also

Elizabeth, who was but "simplish at best." Could they not be spared, he pleaded, "and let the Lord doe with me, and mine, what seems good in his owne eyes."

The General Court responded by passing a bill against witchcraft modeled upon the Jacobean statute. By so doing it fulfilled the first command of the new charter: all laws had to be in conformity with those of England. It also locked the door on spectral evidence first shut by Phips, for the offenses punishable under the law were clear: practicing conjuration, entertaining any evil spirit, taking up the dead from the earth, and using sorcery, whereby any person shall be killed or lamed. Treasure finding and preparing love potions were punishable by one year in jail. Under the statute the Superior Court of Judicature for the colony, its new high court, sent warrants to the towns to choose grand and petty (trial) jurors for a new round of trials.

On January 3 the court met, its bench consisting of Stoughton, Danforth, Richards, Wait Winthrop, and Samuel Sewall. Stoughton ordered those women who had been reprieved "for the belly" (they had been pregnant) prepared for execution, but Phips stayed the order until the Crown signified its pleasure. When word reached Stoughton at the end of the month that Phips had quashed the death sentences, the judge stalked off the bench, fuming that he was just about to "clear the land" of witches when Phips interfered.

Without the admission of spectral evidence, the cases of all but three of the thirty-one accused in January ended in acquittal. Grand juries had indicted them, but trial juries had doubts, and that was enough. The juries had reversed their spring and summer roles, however, the trial juries proving harder to convince than the grand juries. There is no reason given in any of the brief records of the cases why the twenty-eight were discharged or the three convicted. The exclusion of spectral evidence need not have changed the jurors' thinking, for all of them had either seen the girls in action or heard about the specters. A judicial ruling banishing specters from the courtroom could not erase the jurors' memory. What the new rule did was prevent the girls from testifying so vividly, and that may have made all the difference.

We have a little detail on one of these cases. Sarah Duston, a woman of about seventy or eighty years, was confronted with "a multitude of witnesses . . . but what testimony they gave in seemed wholly forreign [i.e., irrelevant], as of accidents, illness, and etc. befalling them, or theirs after some quarrel." Spectral evidence was barred, and the jury "soon brought her in not guilty." There were still a few convictions, however. Sarah Wardwell, who had confessed, was convicted, but there is nothing in her confession that differed from the other Andover confessions except her admission that she was baptized by the Devil. She was contrite and promised not to backslide. Mary Post of Rowley was convicted, for some reason that is not clear. There is no record of the evidence against her. Simpleminded Elizabeth Johnson Jr., Dane's granddaughter, was convicted as well.

The Superior Court of Judicature met again in April, and juries found the remaining five defendants not guilty. John Alden was discharged by proclamation, having previously fled and now returned. Mary Watkins was held over on a charge of slander for accusing another woman of infanticide. In May, Phips emptied the jails and sent the prisoners home, including the three women convicted in January. They and their relatives soon approached the General Court seeking reparations. The petitions dragged on for another two decades, the General Court reversing the convictions, repudiating the trials, and paying off claims to kinfolk of those who were executed. The children of George Burroughs were still filing petitions in 1750. Some of those who fled did not regain lost property because they had committed another crime—jail breaking. It was legal for the authorities to confiscate the property of those who broke jail, in effect penalizing the innocent. Some scholars have argued that certain officials had a financial interest in the property they confiscated. At any rate, when the people who escaped from custody returned, they were acquitted of all charges of witchcraft but could not get back all of their personal belongings.

Apologies

In the seventeenth century the word *apology* had two meanings. The first was to say that one was sorry. The second, closer to the Greek origin of the word, was to explain. As the trials wound down, many who were involved in them began to formulate one or the other kind of apology.

The first was Cotton Mather. At first he had no intention of apologizing, that is, of saying that he was sorry or that he had done wrong. Instead, his first attempt at apology was an explanation in the form of a defense of the court and the judges, and, of course, his own conduct. Now an outsider, replaced as it were by his father in the councils of their brethren, Cotton had to concede pride of place or compete with his father. Cotton chose the latter course. The two Mathers went about Boston together, saw the same events, and came to different conclusions. Unable to criticize the older man, for whom he had genuine affection and respect, yet all but overwhelmed by the rivalry that had naturally arisen, Cotton responded in a creative and forceful manner. He went on with the project of his own book on the trials. Later, in its preface, he wrote that none "but the Father, who sees in secret" knew the troubles that beset Cotton. It may have been an unconscious reference to his own father as well as the heavenly Father. When Cotton did mention those ministers who nibbled or caviled at his work, he described them as "fourteen worthy ministers" and did not mention his father. Indeed, he averred that it was a "slander" to say that he and his father disagreed.

Though he finished writing after his father, with his father's text, or pieces of it, in front of him, Cotton rushed to publish his tract first. The August sermon became the first chapter of *Wonders of the Invisible World,* in which Cotton insisted that witches could become specters and specters could afflict people. He was keeping his promise to

Stoughton to prove that the convictions were justified. Cotton rehashed Perkins and other English writers (ignoring their caution), rehearsed the dangers to which the Devil had subjected New England, including Indian magic, and moaned, "But what will become of this poor New-England after all? Shall we sink, expire, perish, before the short time of the Devil shall be finished?" The Devil, whether tawny or black, made witches "the owners of spectres," and these could give corporal blows to living people. They could steal money and infect the unwary with disease.

If specters had these powers, then the judges were right in their instructions to the jury. But if Cotton Mather believed that specters had these powers, why was he averse to convicting suspected witches upon spectral evidence? The answer is, he was never opposed to it. He admitted that the Devil Himself could take the spectral shape of an innocent person, and that additional evidence was needed beyond spectral display to convict "the Witch Gang." If the only real safety lay in renewal of the covenant with the Lord, walking humbly into His churches, and giving up sin, what of the apparently blameless, the sanctified, members of the Lord's churches in Salem and Andover who were executed for witchcraft? Cotton judged that they were not really saints at all. Burroughs acted through specters, as did Susannah Martin, Elizabeth Howe, and Martha Carrier. In Mather's retelling of their trials, there was no mitigating evidence. He regarded his version as objective and factual, and his unwillingness to accept exculpating evidence was very close to the judges' own refusal to credit the defendants' denials.

Yet Cotton was not easy in his own conscience. Each passing day brought more evidence that he might have been wrong. In mid-October, as he was finishing *Wonders*, he visited confessed witches jailed in Boston to pray and discovered to his dismay that these women, like Martha Jacobs the previous August, were recanting their testimony. Eight of the confessors now related to Cotton that they had forsworn themselves to please the judges, whom they feared, and to prolong their lives. Could he have been wrong? He knew that he was in the thick of the recriminations, and offered:

[F]or my own part, I was always afraid of proceeding to convict and condemn any Person, as a Confederate with afflicting Daemons, upon so feeble an Evidence, as a spectral Representation. Accordingly, I ever testified against it, both publickly and privately, and in my Letters to the Judges, I particularly besought them, that they would by no means admit it; and when a considerable Assembly of Ministers gave in their Advice about that Matter, I not only concurred with their Advice, but it was I who drew it up.

By the middle of 1693, he repeated the litany of his good intentions to all who would listen, albeit in a huffy, wounded voice. Now he portrayed himself as a small, weak, servant of the church of God who only meant to help those who summoned him in their battle against the temptations of the Evil One. So Cotton Mather tried covering his tracks with words. But Mather, who feared the Devil in Salem, could not stop fighting Him in Boston. Despite a shift in public opinion away from further trials, Cotton continued to believe that armies of devils circled Massachusetts. Perhaps the judges made an error in relying on spectral evidence, but if God let the Devil take on Himself the image of innocent men and women, "it would scarce be possible ever to convict a witch." He just could not admit error.

In *A Brand Pluck'd Out of the Burning* (1693), Mather tried once more to bolster his case against the Devil. He recounted the horrors that young Mercy Short endured and linked them to the panic that Salem had experienced. Short had survived an Indian raid on Salmon Falls, New Hampshire, in early 1690 in which her entire family was slain, after which she was carried into Canada and ransomed by Phips. Sent to Boston, she was a servant when she went past Sarah Good's jail cell. When the old woman asked her for tobacco, the young woman refused and almost immediately thereafter fell into fits. The convulsions supposedly caused by the witch led to bouts of delirium, in which Short had complete recall of the Indian raid. She saw the Devil, who at first was black but later became tawny; in other words, like Tituba He went from African to Indian. The Devil and His minions bewitched, then tortured, then starved Mercy. Those who kept vigil saw her pain and heard her shrieking. She carried on monologues with the Devil and plainly feared that she would suffer the same fate as the condemned witches, for she named some of them. Then, overcome with her own emotions, she would "frolick" about and make fun of the ministers who came to save her. In these manic states she could see specters, proof to

Mather than his views had been correct all along. Short also told Mather that she had a good specter who protected her against the evil ones. Mather believed it all and reported it all. We might hazard a guess that Short's personality was fragmenting into "good" and "evil" parts, but it would be unfair to demand that Mather recognize modern ideas of multiple personality. Mather's manuscript broke off abruptly, though Mercy Short continued to have bouts of severe depression, accompanied by hallucinations.

At the beginning of September 1693, Cotton Mather had gone back to Salem to gather material on specters for his planned history of the church in America. Preparing three sermons to give there, he lost his notes, decided that the Devil's agents had taken them, and was delighted to discover that he remembered most of what he intended to say. Thus "the Devil gott nothing." With these thoughts foremost in his mind, he returned to Boston and found "one of my neighbors horribly arrested by *evil spirits*." It was the late afternoon of September 10, 1693, the day after a woman in the neighborhood, long suspected of being a witch, had treated Margaret Rule badly. Rule suddenly fell down and cried out that eight specters had attacked her, directed by a short black man. Fearing that another witch-hunt would begin (Cotton wrote later), Cotton and Increase raced to the scene. If they could intervene in time, Margaret might not make public what rumor had already spread abroad. They visited her regularly after that, pressing her not to believe the promises or give in to the tortures of the Evil One. Around her had gathered a crowd of young people, before whom the ministers, joined by other notables, performed their "service to humanity." Scoffers also barged in, led by Robert Calef, watching the ministers as well as the girl, looking for signs of fakery. Everyone remembered what had happened in Salem, but Cotton Mather had no doubt that Margaret's possession was real.

Over time he learned the lesson of caution. Mather had many years to live and to think about the trials. In the early eighteenth century there were other witchcraft accusations, scares, and even some investigations, but Cotton Mather stayed away from them. He had seen enough of his own frailty and, perhaps because of it, the demise of much of his towering reputation as a student of the invisible world to prefer a wait-and-see approach. Years later, he admitted, at last, that "there [were] errors committed" at Salem.

As Cotton Mather wavered, at times pleading that he had never wanted the excesses that came from the trials and at other times looking under beds and in closets for more demons, Governor Phips began his apology. He too refused to say that he had made a mistake, instead blaming the whole mess on William Stoughton. Aware that Stoughton had stormed off the bench when he received Phips's pardons for the three new convicts and the two women whose executions had been delayed, and also aware that Stoughton wanted his job, Phips decided to strike the first blow against his lieutenant governor. On February 21, 1693, Phips reported to the Privy Council in England that he had depended upon the court of oyer and terminer "for a right method of proceeding" and that it had acted rashly against many people thought to be innocent. He cited Increase Mather's essay, and relying upon it, argued that the Devil had taken the shape of the innocent. Phips's scapegoat was Stoughton, and Phips wrote: "The Lieutenant Governor upon this occasion [of Phips reprieving those in prison] was enraged and filled with passionate anger and refused to sit upon the bench in a Superior Court then held at Charles Towne and indeed hath from the beginning hurried on these matters with great precipitancy and by his warrant hath caused the estates, goods, and chattels of the executed to be seized and disposed without my knowledge or consent." One later commentator, Robert Calef, a Boston merchant turned crusader against the witch-hunters, would report that the governor had acted when the girls accused his wife of being a witch, but Calef was a master of dramatic overstatement.

In the Village, there were no real apologies. Faced with the enmity of many of his parishioners and finally realizing that the witch-hunt was a disaster, Parris decided upon a tactical retreat. His attempt at apology was a combination of blame shifting and concessions of misjudgment. When he finally met with the whole town on November 26, 1694, he turned the tables on his opponents and admitted to having a sore conscience. He had spoken too soon and with too much acerbity in 1692, and had believed where he should have doubted. His "Mediations for Peace," as he styled them, sought a reconciliation. Forgiveness, under the "mantle of love," would repair what had been rent. They were still his "beloved flock." Had the calamity not broken first upon him and his family, perhaps he would have exercised better judgment. He owned his error and apologized to those who had been harmed. He was deluded by Satan, as others were.

There was more self-pity than real contrition in his mediation, something the Nurse and Cloyse families must have recognized. For them, Parris's apology came a little late and was a little forced. Unmoved, they asked for a copy. He refused, unless they gave him a copy of their grievances. It was a replay of the January 1692 confrontation and ended the same way, with both sides retiring, still enemies, to tend their wounds and plan for the next battle. The council of local ministers that met in April 1695 to settle the quarrel suggested that Parris go but refused to condemn him. Instead, its members, led by Increase and Cotton Mather, censured the Village for its factiousness. After a year's additional recrimination, Parris finally left, still unbowed, perhaps even unaware of the damage he had done, his pride—the pride of the master class, a planter's pride—hurt but intact. He found another pulpit, briefly, then returned to a merchant's life, remarried, and had more sons, one of whom he named Noyes in honor of the minister Nicholas Noyes, who stood by him to the end.

Behind him the rawness remained, but not for long. True, the Village was now more than ever before split between two factions looking in different directions. On the Ipswich road, the Porters and Joseph Putnam had firmly cast their lot with the commercialization of the town. The Villagers who supported Parris, often the poorer farmers led by the Putnams, had lost the fight for control of the church but not for control of the future. There would always be a place for farmers in New England. The reintegration of Village life began, like the healing of a long-suppurating wound, its scarred edges still visible. Ann and Thomas Putnam resumed their lives, but neither was healthy. Thomas began selling off his patrimony, including parcels to the Townes family of Topsfield, whose sisters Nurse, Cloyse, and Esty, the Putnams had condemned in the trials. Thomas passed away in 1696, worn out in his forty-sixth year. Ann Sr. soon followed. Thomas's brother Edward was joined by his half brother Joseph, the Putnam who had married into the Porter clan, to administer the estate. A new, young minister, Joseph Green, came to the Village fresh from Harvard in 1697, avoided quarrels, held out the right hand of fellowship, and invited the dissenters to return. Attendance at church increased. Green died in 1715, at age forty, much loved and honored. In 1752 the Village finally became the town of Danvers.

Unlike Parris (who despite his lack of charity was in many ways as much a victim as a malefactor), John Hale, minister in Beverly, had watched the crisis unfold from its inception and could have acted differently had he so desired. Writing about it was hard for him, for he had been an accuser. Giving evidence against Sarah Wildes, executed on July 19, 1692 (no doubt in part because of the weight of evidence like Hale's), he recalled that some fifteen or sixteen years before in Beverly, Goodwife Reddington of Topsfield had come to him to complain that she was bewitched by Wildes. He told the magistrates then, and no doubt the judges at the trial, that Reddington was visited by Wildes's son, who confessed that his mother was a witch. Hale felt no compunctions (nor was his conduct unusual) in passing on stale rumor, hearsay, and unsubstantiated accusation. He was no less a part of the vernacular culture—the network of oral storytelling and information sharing—that sustained the bulk of social intercourse in northern New England.

Gradually, over time, he had seen the error of his ways. In 1697 he composed his own judgment of the affair and left it in the hands of fellow minister John Higginson, who published the account with an introduction when Hale died. Hale confessed, "I have been from my youth trained up in the knowledge and belief of most of those principles I here question as unsafe to be used." It was difficult to disavow these principles, but the events at Salem had led him to question and, by questioning, to discard error. For his conscience was now "tender," and with grief in his heart he acknowledged that the innocent had suffered. Hale began his apology with the same tales that the Mathers had used, but he reexamined them in the light of what later occurred. Hale concluded that false witness and natural causes were responsible for some of the prosecutions, mingled with malice and ignorance among the accusers. For his own part, he begged that some effort be made to repair the reputations and restore the estates of those wrongly convicted and punished.

At the beginning of 1697, the General Court ordered a day of fasting and soul-searching for the tragedy at Salem, the day that many had wanted the General Court to proclaim in October 1692. Deeply moved, and fearing that his own guilt had led to illness and death in his family, Samuel Sewall reconsidered his role on the court. To his minister,

Samuel Willard, Sewall gave a copy of a confession of sin. Willard read it aloud at the fast day, as Sewall stood in silence in his pew, and it was posted on the wall: "Samuel Sewall, sensible of the reiterated stroke of God upon himself and family; and being sensible, that as to the Guilt contracted, upon the opening of the late Commission of Oyer and Terminer at Salem (to which the order for this day [of fasting, passed by the General Court] relates) he is, upon many accounts, more concerned than any that he knows of, Desires to take the Blame and Shame of it, Asking pardon of men." Sewall's piety was deep but conventional. His diary was filled with omens and portents. He believed in witches and feared the Devil. He was also a man of exceeding good sense, a practical man, and he realized, if belatedly, that somehow God's people had gone tragically astray.

William Stoughton never apologized—never said he was sorry or had erred, never even explained himself, except so far as to repeat that he thought the Devil had come to Massachusetts and that witches were hell-bent on doing evil all around. For his recalcitrance, he was rewarded with the governorship, replacing Phips, whose job he had coveted and whose position he had done his utmost to undermine after the witch-hunt had turned into a fiasco. Everyone involved in the crisis was contrite—everyone except Stoughton. He has no defenders.

Conclusion

Can it happen again, in our time? The sad answer is yes, for it has happened over and over after Salem. In Barbados and in Nigeria, Tituba's homes before Salem, witches are still feared and persecuted. In the 1990s suspected witches by the hundreds—the actual number may never be known—were summarily executed by angry neighbors in South Africa. The suspects were older women and men, and the pattern of suspicion and accusation differed little from that in Salem.

The fact is that here and now, in our enlightened time, when the folk beliefs and superstitions of the seventeenth century seem so far away, we entertain superstitions suited to our own fears. They are the folklore of racial prejudice and animosity toward foreigners. They are the folklore of gender-bashing and gay-bashing. And we still persecute witches. A series of cases involving suspected satanic rites has led to trials and convictions. Today there exists a professional class of demon hunters not far removed from the witchfinders of the seventeenth century. These modern diviners go from place to place, holding press conferences and giving interviews in their effort to ferret out and punish those who worship Satan. The world of Tituba, Betty, and Cotton Mather changed after Salem, in part as a result of the tragedy of it, but their sacrifice has not saved us from our worst suspicions of one another.

Such fears are in one sense inevitable. They are part of the frailty of human nature. Choose at random from the available late-twentieth-century examples of the same process—pressure exerted on ordinary people living in an ordinary community to come to grips with the horrifying disturbances of modern life—and one will find rumor leading to fears of a conspiracy. Fear opens the windows of credulity, and fevered imaginations see witches and the Devil. In the winter of 1993–94, gripped by fear of a crime wave, people in St. Louis turned the fact that two girls had been abducted and slain into a grisly (and untrue) tale of satanic rites of dismemberment. Every year at Halloween in Stull, Kansas, in our nation's heartland, ordinary people break into the town cemetery, hoping to catch a glimpse of the Devil—for it is rumored that the burial ground is one of the two gates to hell. The other can be found in Salem.

Yet most of us do not believe in the sulfurous power of the invisible world. We can rise above our animosities and anxieties, our need to blame others for our own failings. Our faith in ourselves, though it may be no more than skin-deep, is, like our skin, a durable protection against most of the claims of the witch-hunters. And history can teach us the dangers of such events.

CHRONOLOGY*

1629	Settlement of Salem (Naumkeag).
1670s–1680s	Salem Village builds its meetinghouse and hires its first ministers; the Porters and the Putnams begin their contest for control of "little politics" in the Village as sentiment grows among some Villagers for separation from Salem town. Young Samuel Parris emigrates to Barbados with his family, attends Harvard College in Cambridge, Massachusetts, returns to Barbados to manage his late father's estate, then removes to Boston to run a shop and preach the gospel. Parris marries, and he and his wife, Elizabeth, have three children.
1684–89	Massachusetts loses its charter and is merged with other New England colonies into the Dominion of New England, but several notables from the old charter Court of Assistants, including William Stoughton and Wait Winthrop, serve in the new government. Nathaniel Saltonstall, appointed to the council, refuses to sit.
1688	War of League of Augsburg breaks out in Europe, pitting England against France; James II is driven from his throne in England and replaced by a Protestant prince from the Netherlands, William of Orange, who will rule jointly with his wife, Mary, King James's daughter.
1689	War comes to New England's frontiers, where it is called King William's War. News of the ascension of William and Mary comes to New England. Anticipating that the new monarchs will sanction their acts, Massachusetts popular party leaders imprison the royal governor, Edmund Andros, and reestablish a charter government. Increase Mather and Samuel Sewall in England plead for restoration of the old charter.
November	Samuel Parris settles in Salem Village with his family and his slaves, Tituba and Indian John, and begins to preach.
1690–91	Tensions in Parris's congregation erupt into open partisanship.

*Adapted from David C. Brown, *A Guide to the Salem Witchcraft Hysteria of 1692* (1984); Peter Charles Hoffer, *The Devil's Disciples: Makers of the Salem Witchcraft Trials* (1996); and Richard B. Trask, *The Devil Hath Been Raised: A Documentary History of the Salem Village Witchcraft Outbreak of March 1692* (1992).

1692

January	Elizabeth Parris Jr. (Betty), middle child of Samuel and Elizabeth, falls ill. Her cousin, Abigail Williams, follows suit, as does a neighbor, Ann Putnam Jr., and many of their friends.
February	William Griggs, local physician, declares that the cause of the girls' maladies is supernatural. Nearby ministers join Parris in prayer for the girls. Neighbor Mary Sibley asks Tituba to bake a witch cake to find the culprit. The girls accuse three local women, including Tituba, of visiting in spectral form and causing their illness. On February 29 the Putnams ask Salem magistrates Jonathan Corwin and John Hathorne to begin an official inquiry, which the magistrates do.
March 1	Tituba, Sarah Good, and Sarah Osborn are examined in Salem Village meetinghouse. Tituba confesses.
March 12	Ann Putnam Jr. accuses Martha Corey of witchcraft.
March 19	Abigail Williams accuses Rebecca Nurse of witchcraft.
March 21	Hathorne and Corwin examine Martha Corey.
March 24	The magistrates hold hearing on Rebecca Nurse and detain her.
Late March	The Proctors are denounced as witches.
Early April	Mary Warren, the Proctors' servant and formerly one of the accusers, admits to lying and accuses the other girls of making up the accusations.
April 11	The Proctors are examined before Deputy Governor Thomas Danforth and other visiting Boston dignitaries.
April 19	Abigail Hobbs, Bridget Bishop, Giles Corey, and Mary Warren are examined. Hobbs confesses. Warren reverses herself and rejoins the accusers.
April 22–May 20	Fifteen more suspected witches from Salem and neighboring towns are examined and imprisoned, including Rebecca Nurse's sister, Mary Esty. Only Nehemiah Abbot is cleared by the accusers. George Burroughs is arrested in Wells, Maine, and examined. Margaret Jacobs confesses and accuses her grandfather (George) and Burroughs of being witches. Sarah Osborn dies in prison.
May 14	Increase Mather and newly appointed governor, William Phips, arrive in Boston from England.

May 20–24	Elizabeth Cary of Charlestown is incarcerated.
May 27	Governor Phips on his own authority constitutes a court of oyer and terminer to hear the witchcraft cases. The court includes Lieutenant Governor William Stoughton, presiding judge, and Saltonstall, Winthrop, Bartholomew Gedney, Peter Sargeant, John Richards, and John Hathorne. Salem lawyer Thomas Newton is selected to prosecute for the colony. None of the defendants will have legal counsel.
May 29	Cotton Mather writes a letter on spectral evidence to Judge John Richards.
May 31	Five more defendants are examined. All are jailed. Among them are Philip English, a wealthy merchant, and John Alden, a ship captain. Both will escape prison and not return until after the trials have ended.
June 2	Bridget Bishop is tried and found guilty. She is executed on June 10. Saltonstall quits the court in disgust and is replaced by John Corwin.
June 15	Twelve ministers ask Cotton Mather to write a letter for all of them to the court asking that spectral evidence not be admitted at the trials. Mather writes the letter but adds a last sentence urging the judges to cleanse the land of witches.
June 16	Roger Toothaker, arrested on May 18, dies in Boston prison.
June 29–30	Rebecca Nurse, Susannah Martin, Sarah Wildes, Sarah Good, and Elizabeth Howe are tried and convicted. They will be executed on July 19. Nurse's demeanor is then so godly that many observers begin to doubt the court's haste. Good is not so well behaved, and tells pro-court minister Nicholas Noyes of Salem that when he dies he "will have blood to drink."
Mid-July	Abigail Williams and other accusers are invited to Andover and there begin to accuse townspeople of being witches. In the end, more Andover women and men than Salem townspeople will be imprisoned for the offense. Boston minister Samuel Willard preaches to his congregation that the trials are condemning innocent men and women.
July 27	The colony's new attorney general, Anthony Checkley, replaces Thomas Newton as prosecutor.
August 2–6	George Jacobs, Martha Carrier, George Burroughs, John and Elizabeth Proctor, and John Willard are tried and convicted.

All but Elizabeth are executed on August 19. She is reprieved because she is pregnant. Burroughs's deportment at the execution is so serene that bystanders begin to demand a stay of the sentence. Cotton Mather rushes to pacify them, and the hanging proceeds.

September 9   Martha Corey, Mary Esty, Alice Parker, Ann Pudeator, Dorcas Hoar, and Mary Bradbury are tried and convicted. Hoar will confess shortly before she was to die and will not be executed, a decision that will ultimately lead to her survival. The others are hanged on September 22.

September 17   Margaret Scot, Wilmott Redd, Samuel Wardwell, Mary Parker, Abigail Faulkner, Rebecca Eames, Mary Lacy, and Abigail Hobbs are tried and convicted, Hobbs, a confessor, is returned to jail. Faulkner, Eames, and Lacy are temporarily spared. Like Elizabeth Proctor, they will be condemned by Stoughton but saved by Phips in January 1693. The others are executed on September 22.

September 19   Giles Corey is pressed to death under stones for refusing to accept the authority of the court.

September 22   After the mass execution, the judges meet with the court clerk, Stephen Sewall, and Cotton Mather, and arrange to lend Mather the records of the trial. He is to write a defense of the judges, which he does, under the title *The Wonders of the Invisible World*. It is published at the end of the year.

End of September   Samuel Willard, defying Governor Phips's gag order against any publication on the trials, writes a condemnation of the trials and circulates it under a pseudonym.

Early October   Increase Mather, urged by the Ministerial Association, prepares his own treatise warning against the use of spectral evidence. Shown to Phips, it convinces him to recess the court and order it to bar spectral evidence in the future. Thomas Brattle writes his own "letter" condemning the trials.

October 12–29   Phips dissolves the court of oyer and terminer and explains himself to the king's advisers in England.

November 25– December 14	Meeting for the second time since Phips returned with the charter authorizing them to pass legislation, the General Court (assembly) of the colony establishes a regular Superior Court of Judicature, which has jurisdiction over all crimes of "life and limb." Witchcraft is made one of these. The court's judges are to be Stoughton, Winthrop, Richards, Sewall, and Danforth.

1693 *(new style—in the old style of dating, which the colonial courts used until 1752, the new year began March 25)*

January–February	The trials of witches resume, but no spectral evidence is allowed. Of fifty-six persons indicted, only three are convicted. By the end of the month, trial juries will convict no one who has been indicted. When Stoughton tries to execute his death warrant for the reprieved convicts, Phips stops the proceedings. Stoughton resigns, promising to have Phips removed from office. Phips makes his second report on the proceedings, blaming Stoughton for the excess of zeal on the court.
Spring	Two more trials, no convictions, and Phips pardons everyone still in custody, including those awaiting execution.
1693–96	Partisanship in Salem Village continues, as Parris is unable to make amends. He leaves for another pulpit.
1696–1700s	The General Court of Massachusetts, responding to petitions by family members of those condemned and imprisoned, begins to vote monetary reparations. Cotton Mather apologizes.

BIBLIOGRAPHICAL ESSAY

The Salem witchcraft trials lasted a year, from June 1692 through May 1693, involved over two hundred suspects, and galvanized the attention of the entire British imperial world. They have also spawned a veritable cottage industry in scholarship, genealogies, and fiction. One of the most recent of these, Peter Charles Hoffer, *The Devil's Disciples: Makers of the Salem Witchcraft Trials* (Baltimore: Johns Hopkins University Press, 1996), provides full scholarly citations for the narrative in the present volume.

The original documents on the accusations, indictments, and trials, along with the dockets and records of the quarterly courts, the later county courts, and the special courts of oyer and terminer are to be found in the Essex Institute Library in Salem, Massachusetts. The Danvers Historical Society and the Danvers Public Library have additional documentary evidence. Exhibits at the Essex Institute and the Peabody Museum, also in Salem, and the restorations, archaeological digs, and surviving houses and farms of the Historical District of Danvers and in historic Salem are living reminders of past times.

Recently published documentary collections on the trials and the surrounding events include Paul Boyer and Stephen Nissenbaum, eds., *The Salem Witchcraft Papers: Verbatim Transcripts of the Legal Documents of the Salem Witchcraft Outbreak of 1692*, 3 vols. (New York: Da Capo Press, 1977); and Boyer and Nissenbaum, eds., *Salem-Village Witchcraft: A Documentary Record of Local Conflict in Colonial New England*, rev. ed. (Boston: Northeastern University Press, 1993). Older collections like Samuel G. Drake, ed., *The Witchcraft Delusion in New England*, 3 vols. [1866] (New York, 1970), and George Lincoln Burr, ed., *Narratives of the Witchcraft Cases, 1648–1706* (New York: Charles Scribners' Sons, 1914), contain excerpts from Deodat Lawson, Cotton Mather, Robert Calef, John Hale, and others who lived through the trials. Similar cases are followed in David D. Hall, *Witch-Hunting in Seventeenth-Century New England: A Documentary History, 1638–1692* (Boston: Northeastern University Press, 1990). Danvers's town archivist Richard B. Trask has prepared the useful *"The Devil Hath Been Raised": A Documentary History of the Salem Village Witchcraft Outbreak of March 1692* (West Kennebunk, Maine: Phoenix Publishing, 1992). The many volumes of George Francis Dow et al., eds., *Records and files of the Quarterly Courts of Essex County, Massachusetts* (Salem, Mass.: Essex Institute, 1911–75), provide a vivid idea of the disorderliness of these pious men and women. David C. Brown, *A Guide to the Salem Witchcraft Hysteria of 1692* (Worcester, Mass., 1984), offers a walking tour of the important places in the trials.

Accounts of the cases began to appear while they were in progress. Notable among these are Cotton Mather, *The Wonders of the Invisible World* (Boston, 1692); Deodat Lawson, *A Brief and True Narrative of Some Remarkable Passages* . . .

(Boston, 1692); Lawson, *Christ's Fidelity the Only Shield Against Satan's Malignity* (Boston, 1693); Samuel Willard, *Rules for the Discerning of the Present Times, Recommended to the People of God in New England* (Boston, 1693); Willard, *Some Miscellany Observations Respecting Witchcraft in a Dialogue Between S and B ... Printed in Philadelphia in 1692* (reprinted Boston, 1869); Increase Mather, *Cases of Conscience Concerning Evil Spirits Personating Men* (Boston, 1693); Cotton Mather, *A Brand Pluck'd Out of the Burning* (Boston, 1693); and Robert Calef, *More Wonders of the Invisible World* (London, 1700). Later generations of Massachusetts writers, beginning with Thomas Hutchinson, *History of the Colony and Province of Massachusetts Bay,* vol. 2 [2d ed. 1768], ed. L. S. Mayo (Cambridge, Mass.: Harvard University Press, 1936), and continuing into the nineteenth and early twentieth centuries with Charles W. Upham, *Lectures on Witchcraft, Comprising a History of the Delusion in Salem in 1692* (Boston: Carter, Hendee, and Babcock, 1831), and Upham, *Salem Witchcraft,* 2 vols. (Boston, 1867); George Lincoln Burr, *New England's Place in the History of Witchcraft* (Worcester, Mass.: The American Antiquarian Society, 1911); and George L. Kittredge, *Witchcraft in Old and New England* (Cambridge, Mass.: Harvard University Press, 1929). Marc Mappen, ed., *Witches and Historians: Interpretations of Salem* (Huntington, N.Y.: R. E. Krieger, 1980), review some of the earlier scholarly accounts of the Salem cases.

Modern scholars have found the cases fascinating for other reasons. They have been used as evidence of larger themes, including the separation between elite and popular cultures, the effect of commercial development on poorer farming families, the role of gender in the colonies, and the capacity or incapacity of early modern legal systems to handle suspicions of crime. Recent books and articles on the trials have included Frances Hill, *A Delusion of Satan* (New York: Doubleday, 1995); Elaine Breslaw, *Tituba, Reluctant Witch of Salem* (New York: New York University Press, 1996); Paul Boyer and Stephen Nissenbaum, *Salem Possessed* (Cambridge, Mass.: Harvard University Press, 1974); Marion Starkey, *The Devil in Massachusetts* (New York: Alfred A. Knopf, 1949); Chadwick Hansen, *Witchcraft at Salem* (New York: G. Braziller, 1969); Larry Gragg, *The Salem Witch Crisis* (New York: Praeger, 1992); Wendel Dean Craker, "Cotton Mather's Wrangle with the Devil" (Ph.D. diss., University of Georgia, 1990); Bernard Rosenthal, *Salem Story: Reading the Witch Trials of 1692* (Cambridge: Cambridge University Press, 1993); and Sanford J. Fox, *Science and Justice: The Massachusetts Witchcraft Trials* (Baltimore: Johns Hopkins University Press, 1968). Enders A. Robinson, a descendant of Sarah Wardwell, one of the condemned witches reprieved by Chief Judge William Stoughton and pardoned by Governor William Phips, recently used family papers to compose *The Devil Discovered: Salem Witchcraft, 1692* (New York: Hippocrene Books, 1991).

Articles on the trials continue to appear as well. David C. Brown has been writing on the Salem events for many years. His articles include "The Case of Giles Corey," *Essex Institute Historical Collections* [hereinafter *EIHC*] 121 (1985):

282–300, "The Salem Witchcraft Trials: Samuel Willard's *Some Miscellany Observations,*" *EIHC* 122 (1986): 207–36, and "The Forfeitures at Salem," *William and Mary Quarterly* 3d ser. [hereinafter *WMQ*] 50 (1993): 85–111. At the conference "Perspectives on Witchcraft: Rethinking the Seventeenth-Century New England Experience" held at Salem on June 18–20, 1992, a gathering of scholars added their insights to the record. These essays were published in successive numbers of the *EIHC* in October 1992 and January 1993. These include Louis J. Kern, "Eros, the Devil, and the Cunning Woman: Sexuality and the Supernatural in European Antecedents and in the Seventeenth-Century Salem Witchcraft Cases," *EIHC* 129 (1993): 3–38; Elizabeth Reis, "Witches, Sinners and the Underside of Covenant Theology," *EIHC* 129 (1993): 103–18; Richard P. Gildrie, "The Salem Witchcraft Trials as a Crisis of Popular Imagination," *EIHC* 128 (1992): 270–85; Alfred A. Cave, "Indian Shamans and English Witches in Seventeenth-Century New England," *EIHC* 128 (1992): 239–54; and Mark A. Peterson, "'Ordinary' Preaching and the Interpretation of the Salem Witchcraft Crisis by the Boston Clergy," *EIHC* 129 (1993): 84–102. One should also read James E. Kenes, "Some Unexplored Relationships of Essex County Witchcraft to the Indian Wars of 1675 and 1689," *EIHC* 120 (1984): 179–212.

The Salem cases came at the end of a century of tensions, pressures, and divisions that led to other witchcraft accusations. On the latter, see Carol F. Karlsen, *The Devil in the Shape of a Woman: Witchcraft in Colonial New England* (New York: Norton, 1987); John Putnam Demos, "Underlying Themes in the Witchcraft of Seventeenth-Century New England," *American Historical Review* 75 (1970): 1311–26; and Demos, *Entertaining Satan: Witchcraft and the Culture of Early New England* (New York: Oxford University Press, 1982); Richard Godbeer, *The Devil's Dominion: Magic and Religion in Early New England* (Cambridge: Cambridge University Press, 1992); David D. Hall, *Worlds of Wonder, Days of Judgment: Popular Religious Belief in Early New England* (Cambridge, Mass.: Harvard University Press, 1990); Lyle Koehler, *A Search for Power: The "Weaker Sex" in Seventeenth-Century New England* (Urbana: University of Illinois Press, 1980); David Thomas Konig, *Law and Society in Puritan Massachusetts, Essex County, 1629–1692* (Chapel Hill: University of North Carolina Press, 1979); Richard Weisman, *Witchcraft, Magic, and Religion in 17th-Century Massachusetts* (Amherst: University of Massachusetts Press, 1984); Amanda Porterfield, "Witchcraft and the Colonization of Algonquian and Iroquois Cultures," *Religion and American Culture* 2 (1992): 103–24; and Jane Kamensky, "Words, Witches, and Woman Trouble: Witchcraft, Disorderly Speech, and Gender Boundaries in Puritan New England," *EIHC* 128 (1992): 286–309.

Secondary sources on the English and European background of the witchcraft cases abound. Some are descriptive, others analytic. For a sample, see C. L'Estrange Ewen, *Witch Hunting and Witch Trials* (London: K. Paul, 1929); Keith Thomas, *Religion and the Decline of Magic* (London: Weidenfeld and

Nicolson, 1971); Brian P. Levack, *The Witch-hunt in Early Modern Europe* (London: Longman, 1987); Joseph Klaits, *Servants of Satan: The Age of the Witch Hunts* (Bloomington: Indiana University Press, 1985); Ann Llewellyn Barstow, *Witchcraze: A New History of the European Witch Hunts* (San Francisco: Pandora, 1994); D. P. Walker, *Unclean Spirits: Possession and Exorcism in England and France in the Late Sixteenth and Early Seventeenth Centuries* (Philadelphia: University of Pennsylvania Press, 1981); Michael McDonald, ed., *Witchcraft and Hysteria in Elizabethan London: Edward Jorden and the Mary Glover Case* (London: Tavistock/Routledge, 1991); Alan MacFarlane, *Witchcraft in Tudor and Stuart England* (London: Routledge and Kegan Paul, 1970); Wallace Notestein, *A History of Witchcraft in England from 1558 to 1718* (New York: Russell and Russell, 1911); Katharine M. Briggs, *Pale Hecate's Team* (London: Routledge and Kegan Paul, 1962); Ian Bostridge, "Debates About Witchcraft in England, 1650–1736" (Ph.D. diss., Oxford University, 1990); Stuart Clark, "Inversion, Misrule, and the Meaning of Witchcraft," *Past and Present*, no. 87 (1980): 97–127; Thomas R. Forbes, *The Midwife and the Witch* (New Haven: Yale University Press, 1966); Alan C. Kors and Edward Peters, eds., *Witchcraft in Europe, 1100–1700: A Documentary History* (Philadelphia: University of Pennsylvania Press, 1972); E. William Monter, *European Witchcraft* (New York: Wiley, 1969); Christina Larner, *Enemies of God: The Witch-Hunt in Scotland* (Baltimore: Johns Hopkins University Press, 1981); and Thomas Harmon Jobe, "The Devil in Restoration Science: The Webster-Glanville Debate," *Isis* 72 (1981): 343–56.

On Parris's life and business, see Bernard Bailyn, ed. *The Apologia of Robert Keayne* (New York: Harper and Row, 1964); Bailyn, *The New England Merchants in the Seventeenth Century* (Cambridge: Harvard University Press, 1955); James F. Cooper Jr. and Kenneth P. Minkema, eds., *The Sermon Notebook of Samuel Parris, 1689–1694* (Boston: Colonial Society of Massachusetts, 1993); Larry Gragg, *A Quest for Security: The Life of Samuel Parris, 1653–1720* (Westport, Conn.: Greenwood Press, 1990); Gragg, "A Puritan in the West Indies: The Career of Samuel Winthrop," *WMQ* 50 (1993), 768–86; Samuel P. Fowler, *An Account of the Life, Character, etc. of the Rev. Samuel Parris* (Salem, Mass.: W. Ives and G. W. Pease, 1857); and Marilynne K. Roach, "'That Child, Betty Parris': Elizabeth (Parris) Barron and the People in Her Life," *EIHC* 124 (1988): 1–27.

On Salem and the surrounding countryside in these years, see Paul Boyer and Stephen Nissenbaum, *Salem Possessed: The Social Origins of Witchcraft* (Boston: Harvard University Press, 1976); George Francis Dow, *Everyday Life in the Massachusetts Bay Colony* (Boston: Society for the Preservation of New England Antiquities, 1935); Claude M. Fuess, *Andover: Symbol of New England, the Evolution of a Town* (Andover, Mass.: Andover Historical Society, 1959); Richard P. Gildrie, *Salem Massachusetts, 1626–1683: A Covenanted Community* (Charlottesville: University Press of Virginia, 1975); Philip J. Greven, *Four Generations: Population, Land, and Family in Colonial Andover, Massachusetts* (Ithaca, N.Y.: Cornell

University Press, 1970); James Duncan Phillips, *Salem in the Seventeenth Century* (Boston: Houghton Mifflin, 1933); A. P. Putnam, "Historical Sketch of Danvers" in *Danvers, Massachusetts* (Danvers, Mass., 1899); Marilynne K. Roach, *A Time Traveler's Maps of the Salem Witchcraft Trials* (Watertown, Mass., 1991); Howard S. Russell, *A Long Deep Furrow: Three Centuries of Farming in New England*, rev. ed. (Hanover, N.H.: University Press of New England, 1976); Harriet Silvester Tapley, *Chronicles of Danvers* (Danvers, Mass.: Danvers Historical Society, 1923); Daniel Vickers, *Farmers and Fishermen: Two Centuries of Work in Essex County, Massachusetts, 1630–1850* (Chapel Hill, N.C.: University of North Carolina Press, 1994); and Christine Alice Young, *From "Good Order" to Glorious Revolution: Salem, Massachusetts, 1628–1689* (Ann Arbor, Mich.: UMI Research Press, 1981).

For answers to questions on law and order in England and New England, see John H. Baker, *An Introduction to English Legal History*, 3d ed. (London: Butterworths, 1971); J. M. Beattie, "Scales of Justice: Defense Counsel and the English Criminal Trial in the Eighteenth and Nineteenth Centuries," *Law and History Review* 9 (1991): 221–67; James S. Cockburn, *A History of the English Assizes, 1558–1714* (Cambridge: Cambridge University Press, 1972); and David Flaherty, "Law and the Enforcement of Morals in Early America," *Perspectives in American History* 5 (1971): 203–56; Flaherty, "Criminal Practice in Provincial Massachusetts," in *Law in Colonial Massachusetts, 1630–1800*, ed. Daniel R. Coquillette (Boston: Colonial Society of Massachusetts, 1984): 191–242; Thomas Andrew Green, *Verdict According to Conscience: Perspectives on the English Criminal Trial Jury* (Chicago: University of Chicago Press, 1985); George Lee Haskins, *Law and Authority in Early Massachusetts: A Study in Tradition and Design* (New York: Macmillan, 1960); Christine Leigh Heyrman, "Specters of Subversion, Societies of Friends: Dissent and the Devil in Provincial Essex County, Massachusetts," in *Saints and Revolutionaries: Essays on Early American History*, ed. David D. Hall, Thad W. Tate, and John M. Murrin (New York: Norton, 1984): 38–74; Adam J. Hirsch, *The Rise of the Penitentiary: Prisons and Punishment in Early America* (New Haven, Conn.: Yale University Press, 1992); N. E. H. Hull, *Female Felons: Women and Serious Crime in Colonial Massachusetts* (Urbana: University of Illinois Press, 1987); Yasuhide Kawashima, *Puritan Justice and the Indian: White Man's Law in Massachusetts, 1630–1763* (Middletown, Conn.: Wesleyan University Press, 1986); John Langbein, "The Criminal Trial Before the Lawyers," *University of Chicago Law Review* 45 (1978): 263–316; Edgar J. McManus, *Law and Liberty in Early New England: Criminal Justice and Due Process, 1620–1692* (Amherst: University of Massachusetts Press, 1993); Louis P. Masur, *Rites of Execution: Capital Punishment and the Transformation of American Culture, 1776–1865* (New York: Oxford University Press, 1989); John Murrin, "Magistrates, Sinners, and a Precarious Liberty: Trial by Jury in Seventeenth-Century New England," in *Saints and Revolutionaries: Essays on Early American History*, ed. David D. Hall et al. (New York: Norton, 1984): 152–206; Emil Oberholzer, *Delinquent*

Saints: Disciplinary Action in the Early Congregational Churches of Massachusetts (New York, 1956); Edwin Powers, *Crime and Punishment in Early Massachusetts, 1620–1692* (Boston: Beacon, 1966); Barbara Shapiro, *"Beyond Reasonable Doubt" and "Probable Cause": Historical Perspectives on the Anglo-American Law of Evidence* (Berkeley: University of California Press, 1991); Joseph H. Smith, ed., *Colonial Justice in Western Massachusetts (1639–1702): The Pynchon Court Record* (Cambridge, Mass.: Harvard University Press, 1961); and Roger Thompson, *Sex in Middlesex: Popular Mores in a Massachusetts County, 1649–1699* (Amherst: University of Massachusetts Press, 1986).

Information on some of the principal actors in the trials can be gleaned from Richard Dunn, *Puritans and Yankees: The Winthrop Dynasty of New England, 1630–1717* (Princeton, N.J.: Princeton University Press, 1962); W. C. Ford, ed., *Diary of Cotton Mather* (New York, 1911); Michael G. Hall, *The Last American Puritan: The Life of Increase Mather, 1639–1723* (Middletown, Conn.: Weslayan University Press, 1988); Everett Kimball, *The Public Life of Joseph Dudley* (New York: Longmans, Green, 1911); David Levin, "Did the Mathers Disagree About the Salem Witchcraft Trials?" *Proceedings of the American Antiquarian Society* 95 (1985): 19–37; Bryan F. LeBeau, "Philip English and the Witchcraft Hysteria," *Historical Journal of Massachusetts* 15 (1987): 1–20; Alice Lounsberry, *Sir William Phips, Treasure Fisherman and Governor of the Massachusetts Bay Colony* (New York: C. Scribner's Sons, 1941); Ernest Benson Lowrie, *The Shape of the Puritan Mind: The Thought of Samuel Willard* (New Haven, Conn.: Yale University Press, 1974); Cotton Mather, *Magnalia Christi Americana, Books I and II* [1702], ed. Kenneth B. Murdock (Cambridge, Mass.: Belknap Press, 1977); Robert Middlekauf, *The Mathers: Three Generations of Puritan Intellectuals, 1596–1728* (New York: Oxford University Press, 1971); Stephen L. Robbins, "Samuel Willard and the Specter of God's Wrathful Lion," *New England Quarterly* 60 (1987): 596–603; John L. Sibley, *Biographical Sketches of the Graduates of Harvard College* (Cambridge, Mass.: Harvard University Press, 1873); Kenneth Silverman, *The Life and Times of Cotton Mather* (New York: Harper and Row, 1984); Silverman, ed., *Selected Letters of Cotton Mather* (Baton Rouge: Louisiana State University Press, 1971); M. Halsey Thomas, *The Diary of Samuel Sewall, 1674–1729*, 2 vols. (New York: Farrar, Straus and Giroux, 1973); Emory Washburn, *Sketches of the Judicial History of Massachusetts from 1630 to the Revolution in 1775* (Boston: C. C. Little, 1840); and David Watters, "The Spectral Identity of Sir William Phips," *Early American Literature* 18 (1983–84): 219–32.

Index